Chronicles of a Spiritual Journey

Stephen Shepherd

Copyright ©2019 by Stephen Shepherd (Higher Ground Books & Media) All rights reserved. No part of this publication may be reproduced may be reproduced in any form, stored in a retrieval system, or transmitted in any form, or by any means (electronic, mechanical, photocopying, recording or otherwise) without prior permission by the copyright owner and the publisher of this book.

Scripture taken from the Holy Bible, King James Version, Copyright 1990 by Thomas Nelson, Inc. All rights reserved worldwide.

Higher Ground Books & Media
Springfield, Ohio.
http://www.highergroundbooksandmedia.com

Printed in the United States of America 2019

Chronicles of a Spiritual Journey

Stephen Shepherd

Breakfast with Superman

John 15:1 "I am the true vine, and my Father is the husbandman."

Theme: There is Only One Supernatural "Man."

I studied for my MFA degree in creative writing at the Vermont College of Fine Arts. At the time—maybe 1987 – there wasn't any internet and few computers. So, most of the back-and-forth correspondence occurred by snail mail, although twice each year for ten days at a time I traveled to Vermont to take face-to-face classes and plan with a writing advisor my work (writing) and reading agenda for the next six months. It was on one of these travels to a winter residency that I met Superman at the Burlington Vermont Airport.

I was sitting at the café counter on the second level eating two eggs over easy with bacon and whole wheat toast when suddenly applause broke out at the ticket counter on the first level below me. It's funny that in public places –especially at airports—that people break into applause when a celebrity enters and is recognized. I had heard this public applause break out at numerous times during my travels at airports, but I was never quick enough to recognize who the applause was for, that is, until that morning at the Burlington Vermont Airport café when Superman suddenly sat down next to me for breakfast at the café's counter.

"How are the eggs?" I heard a voice asked.

I turned my head and there next to me sat Superman—the man of steel who was faster than a speeding bullet.

"You'rrr," I stuttered.

"That's right; I am," he responded nonchalantly. "So, how are the eggs.?"

"Actually, they're pretty good," I said, keeping my composure. "But I'd get the whole grain toast instead of the wheat."

The waitress appeared in front of us, asked for Superman's autograph on a page from her green receipt booklet, and superman ordered exactly what I had suggested—including the bacon, which he had concluded "looked crispy enough."

I talked with Superman for about 30 minutes, with our conversation being interrupted by those people courageous enough to ask for a Superman autograph, and Superman was obliging and kind to all those people who asked. Mostly, the kids just stood and stared in awe at him.

Superman asked where I was going and I told him that after breakfast that I would take a cab alone to the Greyhound Bus Station, and from there the bus would take me the 60 miles to Montpelier where I would spend ten days at the Vermont College of Fine Arts residency. Superman confided that he had flown into Burlington, Vermont to snow ski at Stow and that he was waiting for a limousine that was running late.

We finished our eggs together, me sitting next to Superman, and Superman sitting next to an aspiring writer. And after breakfast, we walked out of the airport together, and then we shook hands and parted. He got into a glimmering black limousine with his beautiful blond-haired wife and her sister, and I got alone into a rent-a-wreck taxi. That day, when I arrived at school, I told everyone about having breakfast with Superman, yet no one believed me. And ten days later, after my residency in Vermont, I arrived home in Iowa to my two children watching Superman on television, and when I told them that I had breakfast with Superman, they didn't believe me either. Now, my children are 40 years old and they still don't believe me. They think that it's just one of the many fantastic stories that I have told them over the years. Frankly, I understand their skepticism because one thing you learn as a writer is that there is very little space between fact and fiction. In fact, whether this story is true or not doesn't really matter, now does it? A good story is a good story, no matter how truthful, and most of the time a good story is a blend of both fact and fiction. Superman is a myth of classic Hollywood proportions because it makes movie-goers believe that an ordinary human being like the man I had breakfast with is capable of superhuman feats like bending steel with his bare hands.

Yet, the guy I spoke with over breakfast that morning was much more human than superhuman. When he visited with me, he was just a regular guy on vacation eating eggs fried over easy for breakfast and looking forward to vacationing with his wife. He didn't pretend to be someone he wasn't. That's because he knew who he was—a mere mortal like all of us who knows the identity of the real Superman.

Questions
1. Who is the real supernatural Superman?
2. Why don't some people believe the supernatural feats of Jesus in the Bible?
3. What is the difference between the superhuman events in the Bible and the Hollywood ones?
4. Isn't it odd that some people will believe the myths of Hollywood over the facts of the Bible? Name some Hollywood characters with make-believe superhuman traits. Then, name some of the superhuman feats performed by Jesus in the Bible.

A Story about Hitchhiking

Acts 6:4 "But we will give ourselves continually to prayer, and to the ministry of the word."

Theme: Prayer is a Two-Way Street

    In the summer of 1967, I was hitchhiking on I-75 on my way home from college. While attending college I couldn't afford a car, so I hitchhiked everywhere. Back then, everybody was hitchhiking; the sides of the Interstate Highway ramps were thick with college students going somewhere, and in general, drivers were not afraid of giving them a ride. Most drivers thought of hitchhikers as amiable college students in search of adventure, and they welcomed their company and conversation.
    On this day with the sun quickly setting, my cardboard sign reading "Detroit" caught the attention of a man driving by in a white Cadillac. When the car pulled over to the side of the road and stopped to let me in, I opened the front seat passenger's door after seeing that the driver was alone. When the front door was opened, the driver told me that if I wanted a ride to Detroit that he would give me one on two conditions: First, I sat in the backseat. And second, I didn't say a word until we reached the exit where I wanted to get out. From where I stood holding onto the front door handle of his Cadillac, Detroit was still 335 miles away, and it was almost nightfall, so I closed the front door, opened the car's rear door, and jumped into the backseat. It was only then that I noticed what the driver was wearing.
    It was July and 89 degrees in the shade, yet the driver was wearing a wool red-and-black checkered hunting suit, complete with hunting hat and downed ear flaps. Then I noticed that the heater in the car was turn up to maximum; it must have been 110 degrees inside his car. But with the sun setting and Detroit still being where it has always been located 335 miles away, I kept my mouth shut, sweated bullets for 5 hours, and probably lost 12 pounds in the car's heat. Eventually, I arrived at my I-75 exit five hours later without uttering a single word of conversation and with only my own

observations on which to tell this story.

Over the next 50 years, some questions about this event have entered my mind: Why was the man dressed in a wool hunting suit in July? Why was the car's heater turned up to 110 degrees? Why didn't the rotund guy in the hunting grab want to talk? And why was I only allowed to sit in the backseat of his car? I still don't know the answers to any of these questions because the man did not want to talk to me. Lately, some other questions have bothered me about this trip like: Did the man drive home to a loving wife who was also a seasonal cross-dresser and wearing an identical hunting suit? Did the man own a meatpacking plant that required him to often enter the cooler? Did the car's heater malfunction and get stuck on hot? Did the man even own the Cadillac that he was driving? These questions, and many more, still haunt me today because conversation is a two-way street, and the Cadillac driver's mouth was closed for construction.

Therefore, a one-way conversation doesn't get information; it only fills the air with one-way questions. It takes two to communicate, and if one person isn't talking then no communication takes place. It is also this way with God. If you don't talk to Jesus, then He probably won't talk to you. And, even if you hear His voice—now and then—you probably won't recognize it. In a friendship, continuous dialogue and trust are the keys to communication. Friends talk to friends differently than they talk to other people because friendship's conversation is more intimate and special. This is how your friendship and relationship should be with Jesus – intimate, special, and genuine. Without these qualities, you might as well be sitting for five hours—sweating and silent— in the backseat of a sweltering Cadillac.

Jesus likes dialogue; He hears billions of people pray to Him each day. Because He is God and we are not, we cannot imagine how He gets it all done. But He hears every single word of prayer from every single person. This doesn't mean that He likes what He hears, but it does say that He will listen if we talk to Him and that He is easily accessible. Despite His willingness to talk to us, we often don't talk to Him. Prayer seems so futile when you're dialoguing with an entity that can't be seen. Because of it, some people give up seeking God's voice because many times it seems like they are talking to themselves. Nothing could be further from the truth; God hears your voice, and to Him it is sweet music because one of His own is returning home. Now, at this very moment, you need to understand the importance of praying to Jesus because Jesus is your mediator with God. "" …no man cometh unto the Father, but by me" (John 14:6). It is only through Jesus that God understands and hears you. Likewise, when God through Jesus speaks to you, you will hear them both through your Holy Spirit.

You have the perfect spiritual and holy sound system built into you, complete with a high-powered, interior headset so that you won't miss a word. But you must be praying to Jesus and listening and waiting for your Holy Spirit to reply. Being a good listener is also a requirement for being in an honest friendship. Therefore, pray to Jesus—especially for your salvation—listen for His voice through your Holy Spirit, and begin your prayerful conversation about salvation and going to Heaven. Because if you don't, it will certainly get very hot for you if you take a backseat in hell.

Questions
1. Name some unanswered questions about encounters in your own life?
2. Can you name some logical explanations for the driver's behavior?
3. Name a circumstance where conversation would have shed light on an issue?
4. Are all encounters with others in life random?

Spiritual Events Around Us

Psalm 107:23-24 "They that go down to the sea in ships, that do business in great waters; these see the works of the Lord, and his wonders in the deep."

Theme: Connecting the Spiritual Dots

    The first time that I saw the movie Forrest Gump with Tom Hanks, I couldn't understand how one person could go through life encountering without recognizing the significance of so many historical events. From the Watergate break-in to George Wallace blocking the door to segregate schools in Montgomery, Alabama, Forrest was oblivious to the historical impact of those events that he was witnessing. Sometimes, when we—like Forrest—can't see the importance of the events around us, we think that God isn't making many significant events and we aren't being made a part of them. But that is not true.
    Case in point, many years ago while an undergraduate student, I worked for the LS&I Railroad on an iron ore dock in Marquette, Michigan. From midnight to 8 am, I rode with the empty ore cars out to the Republic Mine forty miles away, where the empty cars were filled with marble-sized taconite iron ore pellets. Once the empty cars were filled, I rode with them on the 40-mile trip back to the ore dock that extended into Lake Superior. The ore dock was 1,250 feet long and 75 feet high with four railroad tracks. When the train pulling the filled cars approached the ore dock, the engineer would turn the train around and back up the cars onto the track and stop. My job was to go along the ore cars while standing on the two slippery rails and reach down and pull a lever on the bottom of each car to open a trap door to empty the iron ore pellets into a chute that led into the hold of the freighter. It was a dangerous job, standing on the slippery railroad tracks with nothing but darkness between your feet. One slip of a foot could end your life by falling between the rails and into the ship's hold to be smothered by the iron pellets. And one night my foot did slip—even though I had purchased the $40 special leather boots recommended by the railroad company. I was

not new at the job, so I was routinely going about my job of releasing the trap door beneath each ore car. I had probably done it a hundred times. Then, one night it happened. As I reached down to unlock the trap door beneath a railroad car, my left foot slipped off the rail, and I tipped and teetered on the slippery rail like an unbalanced tightrope walker. Then at the last moment before falling in the dark void of the ship's hold, my right foot caught enough traction on the slippery rail to allow me to leap to safety onto the wooden catwalk a few feet away. Fear rose in me in a fraction of a second; it came upon me full throttle in a flowing rush. I stood on the safety of wooden catwalk planks and thanked God for a couple of minutes for saving me while the walkie-talkie in my jean's pocket blared the voice of the locomotive engineer asking me why it was taking me so long. When I regained my composure, I took off my hardhat and wiped the beads of sweat off my brow. Then it hit me that I had come very close to dying, and I then looked down at the ore freighter being filled with iron ore pellets parked beside the ore dock. In the Lord's dim light of early dawn, I could barely make out the ship's name on its hull. The name of the iron ore freighter was: The Edmund Fitzgerald.

Questions
1. Have you ever encountered a short-term incident that eventually had long-term implications?
2. Have you ever met an important person (a political figure, etc.) by chance? Why do you think it occurred?
3. Do you think angels are at work on earth? Explain a personal experience. Do you think an angel was on the ore dock with me that night?
4. Have you ever had a supernatural experience?

Be Prepared

Philippians 2:12 "...work out your own salvation with fear and trembling."

Theme: Your Relationship with Jesus

    Many years ago, an accident occurred at a house behind the university where I taught. The accident occurred in a Cedar Shake bungalow; I had often noticed the bungalow's neatness and the colorful flowers in the flower boxes on my way home from work. On many days, I had seen the owner of the house—a thin, white-haired woman in her seventies—working in her yard. That's why I remembered the house and the woman when I read about the accident in the newspaper.

    According to the newspaper's article, the woman had called upon the gas company on three previous occasions to investigate a gas leak. She had often smelled the odor of gas in her kitchen and wanted it fixed. On at least three previous occasions an employee of the gas company had arrived with a hand-held device to measure the level of gas in the house. On all three occasions, the gas company employee with his hand-held device confirmed that no gas leak existed. The fourth time that the woman smelled the odor of gas in her kitchen, she was reluctant to call the gas company again. After three previous visits without detecting a gas leak, she thought that the gas company might consider her crazy, so she decided not to call the gas company, but instead called her son to have him come over to her house to see if he could smell the odor of gas. That's when while dialing her son's number on the telephone that she absent-mindedly struck a match to light a cigarette and blew up her house. The sound of her house exploding because of a gas leak could be heard for miles. In fact, it shook the six story, brick office building at the university where I was at work across the street.

    At the striking of her match, the woman's house exploded into thousands of pieces, and the force of the blast blew the woman out the house's front door and onto the street, where she lay smoldering and unconscious until an ambulance arrived a few minutes later. Her dog, a white Miniature Poodle, was found one-quarter of a mile away — cinder black and wandering around dazed and confused on the 17th green of a public golf course. A golf foursome had heard the explosion, found the dog, and had put two-and-two together. Evidently, the dog had been blown out of the house by the gas explosion and had sailed through the air one-quarter of a mile onto the golf course, where it had somehow landed safely on the softness of the golf course's plush grass.

Fortunately--and miraculously—both the woman and her Poodle survived the explosion. But it makes the point that no amount of precaution—like the woman telephoning the gas company three times for a gas leak—can give us the ultimate reassurance that our actions are enough to save us from harm. By ourselves, we can do nothing. We need the help of the Lord Jesus to provide for our protection, and we should not take the results of previous warning signs in our life lightly.

Today, many people do not take their relationship with Jesus seriously, although they have been warned time and time again throughout their life to pray to Him daily for their salvation and to read His Word. Even though these same people have been given the opportunity time and time again to repent, they still do not and neglect to investigate the truth about Jesus found in the Bible and at church. In effect, they too—like the woman in the story—are casually playing with fire. Although the warning signs of the fires of hell are clear, people still do not seek their safety through salvation in Jesus Christ. And by not doing so, they too run the risk of being caught up in a spiritual explosion at the end of their life.

Questions
1. Was Jesus ultimately present in the woman's life?
2. Are their dogs and other animals in heaven?
3. What kinds of warning signs do you see in other people?
4. What kinds of warning signs did you see – or do you see -- in yourself?

The Story of Boo-Boo Walking

James 5:16 "Confess your faults one to another, and pray one for another, that ye may be healed. The effectual fervent prayer of a righteous man availeth much."

Theme: Walk Your Life in a Forward Direction

    I once owned a cat named Boo-Boo. He was named by my 5-year-old granddaughter because of what had happened to him. Boo-Boo -- before his accident and his injuries (hence, his name Boo-Boo)—was one of twenty-three cats on my dad's small Michigan farm. Every evening my dad would call for his twenty-three cats and they would all show up, running to eat from a large pan and coming from all directions. My dad fed them dry cat food, moist cat food, and milk that he heated in the microwave to an exact temperature. My dad loved his outdoor cats, and they loved him by catching every mouse within one-half mile. Boo-Boo was a multi-colored cat and as my dad related "a good mouser."
    One afternoon Boo-Boo was sleeping in the farm driveway in the warm July sun, and someone ran over him with their car. My mom, dad, my wife, and I were in the house when we all heard Boo-Boo's wail. My mom identified the sound for us all; I guess it was an all too familiar sound to my parents. My wife and I followed my dad out to the gravel driveway where we found Boo-Boo motionless. Routinely, my dad started walking toward the shed to get a shovel to bury Boo-Boo, and that's when my wife and I scooped up Boo-Boo and drove him to a veterinarian four miles away. The old country vet was familiar with all kinds of animal injuries and how to fix them. An x-ray revealed that Boo-Boo had a broken pelvis, and I thought that was fatal news until the vet explained that a cat can recover from a broken pelvis, although a dog could not. However, for Boo-Boo to recover we would have to house him in a deep carboard box for six to eight weeks so that he couldn't move around too much or jump out of it. Then we could take him out of the box to see if he could still walk.
    We followed the vet's orders concerning nursing Boo-Boo back to health, and eight weeks later we took him out of

the cardboard box, stood him upright, and coaxed him to move to see if he could still walk. At first, Boo-Boo just stood motionless on the kitchen tile, as if trying to remember how to walk. Then suddenly, he started to walk backwards and not forwards, and for nearly a week Boo-Boo only walked backwards. Then, one day he suddenly stopped on the same kitchen tile floor, thought for a moment, and then started to walk forwards.

Likewise, for many people learning how to walk forwards again in life is difficult. Sometimes, it's just much easier to give up—to let yourself walk backwards in old sinful habits—instead of getting the courage and having the strength to give them up and to walk forward again. When all hope seems like it is lost and the walk forward seems too difficult, that's when you need to call upon the Lord Jesus for help. God will never give you more weight than you can carry in life, and Jesus' power through the Holy Spirit can strengthen even the most broken person. Right now, just turn to Jesus and pray for help. There is no reason to walk through a sinful life backward, wounded, and afraid, when you can walk forward in life and be made whole again by the power of Jesus Christ.

Questions
1. Do you know anyone who is going backward in life by being their own worst enemy?
2. What kind of behavior does this person exhibit?
3. Could they reverse their direction by asking Jesus for help?
4. Is it ever too late to walk in the right direction through the strength and guidance of Jesus Christ?

Living in the Attic

John 14:2 "In my Father's house are many mansions: if it were not so, I would have told you. I go to prepare a place for you."

Theme: Temporary Inconveniences on Earth

     When I was an undergraduate in college, there was a university housing shortage. Too many freshman students had enrolled at the university, and the university campus dormitories could not house them all. So, the university granted privileges to junior and senior students to live off campus. However, because of the sudden influx of thousands of new students, the landlords owning off-campus housing were also caught off-guard, for they, too, did not have enough apartments to house the students. There was not enough time to construct new apartment buildings, which many construction-contractors erected over the next few years, so the enterprising landlords did the next best thing—they remodeled old large houses into multi-apartment units. In theory, the short renovation time to convert larger houses into apartments seemed to work; a large house could be easily renovated in a few months into three or four small apartments. But then, greed took over, and instead of the landlords converting these large houses into three or four apartments, they started converting the large houses into six or eight apartments. The result was an apartment configuration that defied logic, and that's where the story of my small apartment in the attic of one of these large houses begins.

    My apartment was in a renovated attic on the fourth floor of a Victorian House. The view from the apartment was only through a tiny window at each end of the attic. But the tiny view wasn't the problem. The problem was how to get to the main hallway that led to the stairway that led to the front door. To get to the main hallway, I had to travel through someone else's bathroom. At the bottom of the steep attic wooden stairs, there was a white wooden door with a hook lock on both sides. If someone was using the bathroom, the door would be locked on the bathroom side and I couldn't exit from my attic apartment. Then, if no one was using the bathroom, yet someone simply forgot to unlatch the hook lock from the bathroom side of the door, then I still couldn't get out of my apartment. Then, if someone was using the bathroom or taking a shower, etc. and forgot to lock the inside door latch, I would sometimes walk into the bathroom unannounced and interrupt them. I tried to remember to knock on my side of the door first to make sure that the coast was clear, but sometimes when I was running late to class, I would forget to knock and just dash through the bathroom while someone was using it. I'm sure that the construction people violated city building code with this blueprint, but the city seemingly looked the other way to accommodate more students at the university.

Luckily, this bathroom-get-to-hallway configuration will not exist when Christians get to heaven. The Lord has reserved a room for each of his saved people in a mansion in heaven. And because God is the greatest construction-contractor in the universe, I suspect that His blueprints will be flawless, just as His blueprints are flawless for those saved people destined to be with Him in heaven. This doesn't mean, however, that while on earth that Christians won't have tough times. In fact, Christians can expect to have tough times on earth simply because they are Christians living in a fallen world. A Christian's difficulties will also occur because of how the world's systems are set up by Satan. The entire system of this world is rigged. All worldly systems—economic, social, and political—are controlled by Satan, and Satan does not like fairness; he likes despair through deception. Justice—as Christians know it--seldom prevails on earth. So, greed prevails along with individual self-interest over what's morally correct.

Just like the chaos of my attic room that was blueprinted by greed, Satan blueprints the path of unchristian people in a fallen world to deliver them to his exit door while he keeps them confused by how they got there. However, this is not the case if you live with the Lord Jesus. "In my Father's house are many mansions: if it were not so, I would have told you. I go to prepare a place for you" (John 14:2). Therefore, God has already constructed and reserved a room for you to live with Him in heaven. His blueprint—called The Book of Life—has your name written in it to reserve your place. So, remember God's eternal room reservation for you in heaven every time your accommodations on earth seem unsuitable.

Questions
1. Describe your worst apartment or house.
2. Who and what makes slum lords exist?
3. Why is your name being in The Book of Life important?
4. What does John 14:2 say about life in heaven?

My Arrival at Senior Citizen Status

1 Peter 5:5 "Likewise, ye younger, submit yourselves unto the elder."

Theme: Respect Your Elders

The announcement of my arrival at senior citizen status happened to me at a Burger King in Janesville, Wisconsin, when the store manager shouted it across the restaurant. He was in the restaurant's far corner amid some disheveled tables and chairs wiping up some lettuce scraps atop a greasy table from a half-eaten Whooper when he spotted me at the cash register paying for a $1.00 cup of black coffee. I had ordered, paid, and was about to turn and make my way to my car in the parking lot when he shouted the arrival of my senior citizenship status across the entire restaurant. About 50 patrons heard his raspy voice yell to the cashier, "Wait a minute! He's a senior citizen; he gets the 20% discount!" The restaurant crowd went silent, and the manager made his way hurriedly to the cash register while hastily bumping into tables and chairs along the way and while all eyes stared at me. It became tomb quiet. Then suddenly, I felt guilty about doing something wrong—like I had just held-up the cashier with a 357 Magnum handgun. But, in retrospect, I had done nothing wrong but age gracefully to arrive at the Burger King that morning to pick-up one cup of black coffee before teaching my college students who awaited me in a classroom across the street. However, when the Burger King manager arrived at the cash register, he was there to set the record straight, whereupon he slapped open the cash register drawer, dipped his hand into the chatter of the dime coin bin, and extended his hand to me with the two-dime discount pinched between his thumb and index finger.

By now, and after the embarrassing stares, I would have paid the manager $10.00 to shut up. In fact, I felt kind of cheap about taking the two dimes; I was still working full-time, and I saw no need for the discount. However, the manager had other ideas, and he just stood there looking at me and holding out the two dimes. For 20 seconds we stood in the restaurant's silence -- the tension as thick as a double cheeseburger. Then, I looked around the silent room, saw the nods of approval and the smiles on the other patrons, as if to say, "What are you waiting for? Take the 20 cents; you've earned it." So, I took the 20 cents from the manager's fingers and dropped it into a clear plastic donation container on the counter next to the register. To be honest, to this day only God knows what charitable organization received my 20 cents, but I couldn't keep it. I felt like the Holy Spirit was telling me that it wasn't mine, not yet anyway, although we will all reach a sunset day with the Lord when the 20 cents discount will certainly come in handy.

Questions
1. Explain some incidents in your life when good intentions seemingly turned out bad?
2. Name some other age-related benchmarks in life?
3. What does scripture say about how to treat the elderly?
4. By contrast, how does our culture treat the elderly?
5. How are the elderly treated in other countries like China?

Do-It-Yourself

John 14:6 "I am the way, the truth, and the life: no man cometh unto the father, but by me."

Theme: Salvation Comes only through Jesus Christ

    I once knew a man with a Ph.D. in Psychology who taught at a major university. He was tall, blond-haired, handsome, and quite full of himself. He was so egotistical that he had convinced himself that he was so smart that he could do anything. One day he decided to build his own house. He bought two acres of wooded property and a *Reader's Digest Do-It-Yourself Book* and set upon the task. "How hard can it be?" he said to me one day. "It isn't rocket science!"
    In his spare time, on weekends, and during summer vacation, John spent the next three years constructing by himself his own house in the woods by following the instructions set forth in the *Reader's Digest Do-It-Yourself Book,* which he said contained everything you needed to know about house construction from establishing electrical wiring to pouring concrete. Three years later when the house was finished, he threw a huge house-warming party to showcase his construction work. The party was attended by all 70 members of the university's Psychology Department as well as by family and friends. My fancy invitation arrived in the mail one month prior to the house-warming event.
    On the day of the event, I drove up to John's house and marveled at its appearance. His huge contemporary-designed house was set high upon a hill and had a long, winding driveway leading to it. As I approached the house, I noticed that he had left a huge Maple Tree growing in the middle of his living room; it's trunk and branches protruded from the rooftop. The Maple Tree stated a lot about John's personality; he wasn't one to follow convention. If he wanted a Maple Tree growing in the middle of his living room, then he would have one despite it being an architecturally unsound idea.
    The house-warming party was joyous, and everyone was impressed by John's house construction, and John ate up the kudos delivered from his guests like chocolate-covered mints.

After the house-warming party, I didn't see John for a long time. He had taken a sabbatical to write a book—one that according to him that only he could write. Then, one afternoon I spotted him sitting at an outdoor café table drinking a cup of coffee, and I sat down across from him at the table to chat.

"How is the house?" I asked, thinking that it was his pride and joy.

"Not so good," he replied with a stern look.

"What's the matter?"

"Well, he continued, "right now, it's sliding off the hill. It has something to do with the roots of the Maple Tree being in the middle of the living room."

I didn't see John again for quite some time, so I decided to drive out to see the condition of his house. When I had spoken with him months earlier at the café, he was confident that he could stop his house from sliding off the hill. Yet, when I arrived at his house, it had indeed slid off the hill and was now only so much splintered lumber at the hill's bottom. I thought -- so much for ego and innovation. Not long after his house had moved, John, himself, moved too into a small apartment near campus; it was right after the insurance adjustor wouldn't honor his insurance claim because he had not used professional and bonded contractors to build his house.

Many do-it-yourself people exist today, and the attitude of do-it-yourself even extends into the realm of saving your own soul. Of course, Jesus is the only path to salvation, but that doesn't stop people from performing strange rituals to try and accomplish the task by themselves. They try everything from interpreting patterns in the clouds to reading the bumps on your head. Some people -- like John and the self-building of his house – have constructed such lavish egos that it prevents them from seeing the truth: That there is no substitute for a professional, and when it comes to saving your soul, Jesus is the only contractor to hire.

Questions
1. Name some other ways that do-it-yourself people try to save their soul?
2. Describe a do-it-yourself soul construction project that went bad.

3. What is it called when you construct a conversation with Jesus?
4. How can reading the Bible construct a better life for you?

Auto Accident

Acts 1:7 "It is not for you to know the times the seasons, which the Father hath put in his own power."

Theme: You Never Know the Time

On a soft and sunny Saturday morning in July and under a cloudless blue sky, my wife and I were driving to a friend's house on a 4-lane highway. It was still early by Saturday morning standards—maybe 9 am. The traffic was light, and the 50 miles had started slowly and deliberately with the promise of a leisurely drive and conversation. Then, ahead of our car about one-quarter of a mile away, I saw a traffic pattern that didn't look right. I remember saying aloud to my wife "that doesn't look right." And then, it happened. Up ahead, a black pick-up truck was in the left lane passing a car traveling in the right lane. Then, a car from a side road on the right drove out onto the 4-lane to cross it to get to the center median. The car crossing the highway made it past the car traveling in the right lane, but never saw the truck in the left lane passing the car. This resulted in the truck slamming into the driver's side of the car crossing the highway. Instantly, plastic parts from both vehicles were flying hundreds of feet into the air as the truck t-boned the car. The impact shoved the truck into the opposite, on-coming lanes across the center median, where it came to an abrupt stop. Fortunately, no other cars were coming head-on. The car crossing the highway that was t-boned on the driver's side was forced down into the grassy ditch between the center of the four lanes.

I stopped my car on the right side of the highway and dialed 911 on my cell phone to report the accident. A moment later a radio dispatcher answered. I quickly told her about the accident and its location. And then, she asked me some unexpected questions.

"How many people are in the car?" she asked.

"I don't know," I answered. "I'm still sitting in my car, and the car in the accident is a couple of hundred feet away in the ditch."

"Well, get out of your car and go look!" she growled.

"I don't want to look in the car," I said. "I'm just calling in to report the accident."

Then she asked me the question that finally got me to look inside the car: "Are there any children in the car? We need to bring other equipment if there are children."

"Okay, I'll go look," I replied.

I climbed out my car and ran across the highway over to the grassy center median where the T-boned car rested. I purposely looked into the back seat first to see if there were any baby car seats. I was still on the cell phone with the radio dispatcher.

"No children in the back seat," I reported.

"How about the front seat?"

Thus far, I had avoided looking into the front seat, but then I had to look. A young blond-haired woman, her face and hair covered with blood, was semi-conscious and moaning in the front seat. The young male driver was silent and slumped over the steering wheel.

I reported what I saw to the radio dispatcher, and I remained on the cell phone with her until the ambulance and rescue team arrived five minutes later. After they arrived, my wife and I left. The next day, the newspaper reported the accident and that the man driving the car had died from his injuries. Since then I have often reflected upon how such a simple mistake had ended the life of that man and had forever etched the memory of the accident into the woman's mind. On that quiet Saturday morning with the grass wet with dew and under a cloudless blue sky, I have often wondered where the couple was traveling. Perhaps they were traveling to the lake for a picnic or to his mother's house for a pancake breakfast. I will never know, but no doubt, they were also relaxing on that Saturday morning because the sky was so blue and the sun's rays so soft. In fact, the weather was so perfect that it was almost hypnotic.

People are hot-wired to believe—especially when they are young—that they will live forever. Death—at least for the time being—never enters their mind. This isn't the case for the aged; I'm sure that they think more often about their own mortality. But when you're young you seem almost oblivious to your own eventual demise, and you often go about your life in a reckless fashion that almost translates into an invincibility. As evidence by my narrative about the car accident, your life can end in a fraction of a second. In fact, your actions don't even have to be the death-defying attempts of a dare devil. You can be just walking to the bakery to buy a cake donut and then get hit and killed by a passing ice cream truck.

The point is this: No one can stop your death, but you can take precautions by living your life as safely as possible, but when it is your time to die; it is your time to die. Therefore, it is always important at any moment to be right with God because you don't know the time or the season of your own death, and you should always be ready. And in being ready, you should also remember that God gave you your life, and He can also take it away.

People approach death in two ways. For non-believers, death is totally final. They will no longer speak to the person again or hear their voice. A void on earth will be left by their departure, and grief has no comfort or hope. For the believer and Christian, however, death is not final. It is final in the sense that someone is departing from the earth and will never be seen on earth again. However, death is not ultimately final for the Christian; it is more of a transition from life in this world to life in the next world with Jesus. If you're saved and reborn as a Christian soul, you do not die when your physical body on earth dies. To a Christian, when your physical body dies, your spirit leaves it and goes to live again as a spiritual body in heaven with Jesus. In short, the physical body at a funeral home is no longer you; at the instant of your death, your soul moves on to heaven. For a Christian, the physical body is not your essence; it is only housing your soul—which is your essence. Therefore, the physical body is only your earthly shell, and you—and the essence of you—has already departed to live again with Christ before the funeral. A funeral for a Christian is sad because of the loss of an earthly companion, but it is also a celebration because a Christian soul has already moved on to heaven to live with Jesus. Therefore, physical death for a Christian is not the end of life, but the beginning of a new spiritual life in heaven.

These are the two perspectives on physical death; the nonbeliever's perspective is final and earthly, and the believer's perspective is not final and heavenly. The Christian's perspective is very hopeful, while the nonbeliever's perspective is hopeless. The key to a Christian's hope is belief and faith in Jesus Christ as your Savior. He will save your soul, if you genuinely ask Him! You don't have to be only the physical body that the gravediggers will bury in the ground. With salvation, your soul can leave that physical body and the grave's destination and soar high above the doubts and sadness, and your death can be a time of spiritual renewal in a new life with Jesus. Genuine Christians are not afraid of physical death because they know that another and better spiritual life exists beyond the grave. It is a spiritual life with Christ in heaven, a life without pain and suffering, and a life with friends and family who you will see and recognize again. That's right! You will recognize and meet other Christian family members and friends who have passed when you get to heaven. It a joyous heavenly reunion, and one reunion that you can't afford to miss.

"The hour is coming, and now is, when the dead shall hear the voice of the Son of God: and they that hear shall live" (John 5:25).

Questions
1. When can a funeral be legitimately sad?
2. What does a nonbeliever think about death?
3. Where does a nonbeliever's soul go after physical death?
4. Why is it important to approach friends and family about getting the facts about salvation?

Imperfect Pursuits

John 14:27 "Peace I leave you, my peace I give unto you...."

Theme: A Permanent Solution to Sadness

My dad loved cars; he could never see enough of them. One would pass him on the highway, and he would immediately zoom into a story about how he used to own one. Some of his car stories were very convincing, but if he had owned all the cars that he told a story about, he would have to be Henry Ford. I can still see the smile on my dad's face just before he broke into one of his car stories. Most times, he'd be at the kitchen table with a can of Stroh's Beer in front of him and a Lucky Strike burning down between two of his yellow fingers. Then he'd lean back in his favorite kitchen chair—settle down a bit—then he burst into the tale about when he owned his best car -- a 1948 Mercury sedan. "Fastest car ever made in the United States," he'd say, with a nod overtaking the seriousness of his statement.

"One time," he continued, "I took it down to the new Ohio Turnpike; they'd just finished a new 50-mile asphalt stretch that summer, and I wanted to see what the ole Mercury's four barrels could do. You see, when I stepped down on the Mercury's gas pedal, the first two carburetors would kick in until I got to around 50-55 miles per hour. Then the other two barrels would kick in—that's where you got your 4 barrels from-see? When all four barrels were working, that burgundy Mercury's acceleration would pin you back in your car seat and snap your neck like a 300-pound Chiropractor. Once the Mercury hit 60-65, I could see the needle on the gas gauge moving downward because the engine was sucking so much gas. I didn't mind it at the time, though; in 1946 gas was 10 cents a gallon, and I was in high cotton, making $125 a week working on the assembly line at the Tecumseh Products Corporation. So, I could drive my Mercury anywhere and anyway I wanted.

Today, it would be too expensive to drive that Mercury; you couldn't drive it around the block without filling up the gas tank. I bet it only got 8 miles to the gallon when I was driving it wide open. Maybe I'd hit 125 to 130 miles per hour before backing it off—slowing down to let its dual chrome tailpipes pop like the Howitzers on Guadalcanal. But then, every WWII veteran's car sounded like an exploding hand grenade. It was a type of therapy; we all drove like there was no tomorrow. Now-a-days the car's noise pollution would cost me plenty. Maybe $350-$500 for each pop coming from the tailpipe of a backing-down engine. I'd still drive it today like hell though; it would be worth the cost of the speeding and noise pollution tickets just it to hear the blast of those Mercury's tailpipes firing off just one last time."

Sometimes people are remembered by the stories that they tell. Yet, while the previous story is about a car, it is more about the man behind the car than the car itself. And that's an important point to remember about life: what's presented as the focus of an event, often has a more important underlying meaning. The real story is about a WWII veteran who has returned home from the war's violence and trying to adjust to the world's silence by driving fast and noisy cars. His driving is dare-devil reckless, and he knows it, but he doesn't care because it helps him to temporarily forget about the war.

Today, many people try to forget about their private wars by substituting worldly pursuits. In the previous story, it was my dad's love for cars and his endless pursuit of the car that would satisfy his need to forget. Yet, the only satisfaction one can get on earth from forgetting their past and emerging into a new life is through Jesus Christ. Seeking the Lord's forgiveness and being given His gift of salvation is the only way to remove yourself from your past life.

For years, my dad told stories about cars and sought out new cars as a way of filling the void left by the war. And to his dismay, he never really found the perfect car—the one that would make him completely forget. At times, the brightness of a new car would bring him some temporary solace, as he washed and waxed it in our driveway. But that car too would eventually get old and rust and he would become disillusioned by the way it looked, so he would start searching for another car to fill its place. Of course, he had fun searching for, finding, and then driving a new car, but it never permanently replaced his past life and his bad memories from the war and the sadness that accompanied them.

Questions
1. What worldly things are you pursuing to fill the void in your life?
2. How long does this joy last?
3. What is the only permanent solution to stepping away from your past?
4. How can you start today to be permanently healed in your search for happiness?

Unable to Keep a Job

1 Timothy 6:10 "For the love of money is the root of all evil."

Theme: Honesty

    As a young man, I was never any good at keeping a job. For years I thought that it was my fault until Jesus showed me differently. My first part-time job was working at a shoe store. At the shoe store, I washed windows, vacuumed the floors, restocked shelves, and occasionally waited on a customer. Another high school colleague, Ted, had been working there for over one year. It was a boring job, but as a teenager I had grand plans for all the money that I would earn. That is, until Ted confided in me that the owner was intentionally selling infant baby shoes in the wrong size to reduce store inventory. In short, the owner was selling the shoes he wanted to sell, rather than the correct shoe size that the baby needed. The next day a young couple with an infant son entered the store, and the owner did exactly what Ted had said the previous day. I confronted the shoe store owner in front of the young parents about the incorrect size of the baby shoes and the health risks of a baby wearing the incorrect shoe size. For keeping him honest, he promptly fired me.
    A little while later, I was working in a men's clothing store. Again, I was hired to wash windows, vacuum floors, restock inventory, and occasionally wait on a customer. One day, I was in the clothing store's basement retrieving the vacuum cleaner, when suddenly a city water pipe burst and started flooding the basement with water. The basement was full of metal shelving containing all the store's inventory, and I was quickly removing the inventory from the lowest shelves and placing it on the stairs to protect it from water damage. The store owner heard my shouts for help and came bounding down the basement stairs to see the flooding basement. He waved me away from the shelves, and then he started tipping the metal shelves over onto the floor and into the water. He said that the store's insurance would reimburse him 100%. He then asked me to help him tip over the remaining shelves, and I refused. That's when he fired me.

My next job was being a dishwasher one summer at a local college cafeteria. Again, my job didn't last long. Of course, being a dishwasher isn't very glamorous; it's a behind-the-scenes kind of job. Even at age 15, I was not one much for the limelight; I usually kept to myself. Then, after a few weeks of washing pots and pans by myself in the four stainless steel sinks facing the back wall of the college's kitchen, I looked behind me to the kitchen at 2:30 one afternoon and noticed that I was the only person working. The other four student employees were gone. The small college had a good-faith policy on recording your own time on your timecard for the week. I walked over to the timecard rack, and the missing employees were still punched in. I told the cafeteria manager about it, and I was promptly fired along with everyone else.

Next, I started work as a part-time custodian at a university. The university always tried to hire local high school students when possible in hopes of getting new high school recruits to enroll there. Mostly, I just mopped the long tile hallways in the Student Union. The hallways stretched for miles, and for two months I saw only two other student workers mopping the hallways with me. Then one Saturday morning while mopping the floor at the loading dock, I watched a coach punch in and take away twenty-five timecards from the timecard rack. Four hours later, the coach returned to punch out the twenty-five timecards and replace them in the timecard rack. I later found out that the twenty-five timecards belonged to university athletes. In short, they were getting paid for not working, and I was doing all their work. I complained to the Student Union Manager and asked for an hourly pay raise, and he promptly fired me.

My ill-fated work history would go on and on, but the same theme seemed to resurface every time: Dishonesty pays dividends and honesty does not. In a world controlled by Satan, where money and power are more important than ethical behavior, being fired in a fallen world by my early employers now makes sense because of my present with Jesus. Obviously, they had accepted and applied Satan's sliding scale of ethics. Satan says that the difference between right or wrong depends on whether it benefits you and whether you get caught. For example, it's okay to cheat, lie, and steal if it benefits you and you don't get caught. However, once you accept Satan's ethical relativism, it starts you on a slippery slope morally downward. Each time you make an unethical decision, you compromise a little more of your soul. And, over time, if you continue to make unethical decisions based on Satan's relativism you will eventually become morally empty. Moral behavior, like everything else in life, can be drained from you over time. In fact, moral character is a simple plus or minus equation. Doing the right thing adds to your moral character, and doing the wrong thing subtracts from your moral character. And what to do and how to act morally can always be found in the Bible. In fact, the Bible will fill you to the brim with good character, if you read it.

You would expect in Satan's fallen world that some people would make bad moral choices, but just because it will benefit them and no will know doesn't make a bad decision the right one. God, of course, sees everything you do. By deciding to follow the fallen crowd in a fallen world, you are supporting Satan's efforts to increase evil in the world. No moral decision should be based on personal gain or relative circumstance. Abortion, for instance, is still evil—whether it's partial or full.

Questions
1. Did you ever have a job where unethical practices caused you to quit or get fired?
2. When you complained, did your co-workers defend you?
3. What does the expression "Go along to get along" mean to a Christian?
4. Explain a work situation where employees were unjustly paid for doing little or no work.

The Story of Loopholes

Revelation 22:19 "And if any man shall take away from the words of the book of this prophecy, God shall take away his part out of the book of life, and out of the holy city, and from the things which are written in this book."

Theme: God is the Perfect Author

    A "loophole" is a term related to something that is unintentionally missed. A loophole in a written policy, for instance, means that someone forgot to address an issue that someone else eventually discovered. We all like to be as thorough as possible, especially when writing. However, because we are fallible humans and we often make mistakes, sometimes we are not as thorough as we would like to be, and this gives rise to people who like to exploit loopholes.
    I met my first genuine loophole person while I was a sophomore in college and living in the dormitory. I didn't know much about him, except that he was a male and lived somewhere in a four- dormitory quad that converged on one mutual cafeteria. I only noticed him because of his bizarre dress, and then one day a dorm acquaintance explained his odd appearance to me. It seems that the loophole person wanted to be kicked out of the dormitory because he disliked the lack of privacy and the cafeteria food. Therefore, the loophole person searched the University Dress Code Policy regarding attire when eating in the cafeteria, and this is where the loophole person found his loopholes. The Student Dress Code Policy Manual was woefully inadequate, and he took advantage of the Policy Manual's unwritten loopholes.
    The loophole person's plan went something like this: If a specific article of clothing was noted in the cafeteria policy for student dress code, he would wear it. However, if an article of clothing was omitted from the policy—thus providing him with a loophole—he would not wear it. So, if the policy stated that all students must wear a tie to eat Sunday dinner, then he would show up in the cafeteria wearing a tie but not wearing a shirt. If the policy stated that all students must wear socks, then he would show up wearing socks but no shoes. If the

policy stated all male students must wear a button-down shirt, then he'd wear a button-down shirt but no pants. The loophole person's attire was completely legal according to the University's Dress Code Policy, and he used every meal to drive home that point. Eventually, the university's administration granted him permission to live off campus.

Fortunately, if you read the Bible regularly and you read it closely, you will not find any loopholes. In fact, you would expect a book written by God to be infallible and true, and it is. People who think that the Bible has loopholes are the ones who don't read it or the ones who only read it occasionally and have only a superficial knowledge of it. For others, like those believers who read and absorb the Word of God every day, it has become the essential Instruction Manual for Life. The beauty of the words written in the Bible stems from the fact that each parable, event, and word are multifaceted. Therefore, a one-time surface reading will relay information, but a closer reading will reveal the wisdom of underlying nuances as well. That's why close readers of the Bible can read it time and time again because new wisdom and richness is revealed each time that it is read.

Admittedly, before I started reading the Bible, I had become bored with human literary authors who were influenced by previous authors. Upon close reading of one author, I could see the previous influences of another. This is not the case with the Bible's author—God. God's work is 100% original, and there has never been anything written like it before or since. In literary terms, the Bible is an epic because it contains all the literary plot conflicts available. You wouldn't expect God to write a trite plot and something unimaginative because God is the creator and originator of all things, including you! So, there aren't any loopholes in the Bible, no quicksand for the person seeking a loophole. Everything in the Bible is air-tight and true. In fact, the Bible is very specific about how people should live their lives according to God, and the consequences for not doing so. For example, there is only one pathway to God, and it is through His Son Jesus Christ. This is a fact and one that Jesus so states: "I am the way, the truth, and the life: no man cometh unto the Father, but by me" (John 14:6). So, that statement closes any doctrine loopholes. To arrive at God's side, you have only one way to get there—through Jesus Christ.

This fact is very specifically stated in the Bible, and other statements like this one make it clear that it was not God's intention when He wrote the Bible to create ambiguity. God's intention was to give the reader of the Bible unequivocal knowledge and direction in how to live their life. Unlike the loophole student in my college dormitory cafeteria who read the Dress Code Policy and found loopholes to game the system, no one can game God's system because God is the system.

However, there are differences in perspective about whether the Bible is fallible or infallible, and they depend on who wrote the Bible. If man wrote the Bible as inspired by God, then the Bible is fallible because man is flawed and makes mistakes. This man-written, but God inspired, perspective is doctrine in some religions. If man wrote the Bible, and man is flawed, then logically the Bible is also flawed. However, if you believe—like I do—that the Bible was authored by God and God used man as a conduit to record it, then the Bible is infallible because God is the author and He is incapable of making mistakes. The outcome in both perspectives is very different. One suggests that some men, for whatever reason, were selected by God to write His message, although God didn't write it Himself. This perspective could lead to error and misinterpretation by man as the transfer of the information takes place. On the other hand, if God wrote the Bible directly through man and moved and controlled man's thoughts and literally moved the pen, then there wouldn't be any misinterpretations.

All serious writers know that at times God literally controls the pen and moves the thoughts forward without the conscious will of the writer. Anyone who has written for a long period of time has had their pen hijacked by some force other than themselves. When this occurs, it is like the writer is not writing, but the words are being written and moved for him by some other force. In this case, the writer does not have to think about what is being written; the words just flow and are written down on the page for him, as if the writer is a participant and not the originator of the work. In this case, the writer becomes secondary to the action like he is receiving dictation and not thinking or creating the words himself. However, when the writer consciously chooses words and establishes context in the man-written Bible, loopholes can occur. In the infallible Bible, however, the writing is controlled by an outside power (God) who exerts the force and dictates to the writer what to say.

It makes sense that if God is the author of the Bible and He is the creator of everything perfect, then why would He delegate the most important document on earth—the Bible—to an imperfect man in a fallen world to write? Why would He allow His message to be plagued by the fallible possibilities and inaccuracies of man's judgement, when He could simply make an infallible document Himself just like all His other perfect creations? Human nature has always been flawed, just ask Adam and Eve. By knowing that man is flawed in a fallen world, why would God turn over the keys to the Bible to a bad driver with limited experience? He wouldn't, and He didn't! That's why God wrote His own Words in the Bible for man to read because He knows that the fallible nature of man won't ever let him do anything perfect, much less be the author of the most perfect document on earth.

Therefore, when I read the Bible, I accept what is says because I believe that it is written by God. I don't try to second guess its statements or grapple with unintended meanings. I read, learn, and absorb. For instance, when God states in the Bible that an "unknown disciple" outran Peter to Jesus' tomb, I assume that God didn't tell us the name of the unknown disciple because He didn't want to. I accept the words "unknown disciple" without questioning it or speculating on the most likely identity of the unknown disciple. To me, "unknown" means "unknown," and if God had wanted to tell me otherwise, He would have supplied me with the name of the disciple. Furthermore, man's speculating on the identity of the unknown disciple doesn't make it true; thus, my mindset is that infallible God didn't omit the name of the unnamed disciple by mistake; it isn't a loophole. He simply and intentionally left out the unnamed disciple's name. For me, this unwavering, straightforward, and trustworthy approach to reading God's Word in the Bible dispels all doubt. I am a trusting reader of

God's infallible Word, and it makes my journey through the Bible even more reassuring.

Questions
1. What is your opinion about the authorship of the Bible?
2. What version of the Bible do you read? (KJV, etc.)
3. Does the version and its translation matter?
4. If yes, why? If no, why not?

Chopping Up the Telephone

Matthew 6:19-21 "Lay not up yourselves treasures upon earth, where moth and rust doth corrupt, and where thieves break through and steal: But lay up for yourselves treasures in heaven, where neither moth nor dust corrupt, and where thieves do not break through nor steal: For where your treasure is, there will your heart be also."

Theme: Appearances Are Deceiving

When I was a college undergraduate student, I went home for a weekend to Detroit with a friend. His father owned a plastics company, which he had founded and built. For my friend's father, his company was an idol that he worshipped 24/7. My friend's house turned out to be a mansion in a fashionable Detroit suburb, and upon meeting his father, I was impressed by his businessman's composure. Then on Saturday afternoon while we were eating lunch at the kitchen table, the telephone rang. This was before cell phones, and his father stood up casually and walked across the kitchen to answer the telephone. It was a landline telephone, so it was attached to the wall. He answered the telephone with a polite "hello," which was instantly followed by an outburst of yelling and screaming. In a flash, his confident businessman's composure had turned into a psycho's rant punctuated by numerous swear words. Finally, he slammed the telephone's receiver down to disconnect the call, and I thought that his rant was over. That's when he suddenly ripped the telephone off the kitchen wall and took it outside to the backyard, where he chopped it up with an axe at a place designated for splitting firewood. I looked at my friend, and he seemed unalarmed by his father's actions. Then he calmly said, "Third phone this month."

I have often heard nonbelievers sarcastically comment about the large number of people in Jesus' time possessed by evil spirits. It seems that everywhere that Jesus travelled that He encountered people possessed by the devil. It's true that Jesus did heal many physically and spiritually ill people, but I doubt whether there were more people possessed by the devil back than there are today. The actions of a possessed person back then might have been more apparent to others because of the absence of prescription drugs and psychiatrists, although the increasing number of psychological diseases added recently to the *American Psychological Association's Manual* for diseases seems to indicate that even drugs and counseling aren't stemming the tide of world madness. Today, Satan's fallen world seems to be falling on more and more people with a greater weight and louder thud. You can hear the loudness of the thud when the lives of people hit rock bottom. The stories about their lives aren't pretty: drug and alcohol abuse, infidelity, greed; it's evident that fewer people can cope with the weight of a fallen world's stress. This lack of coping with the stress comes as no surprise because more and more people are turning away from Jesus Christ.

When things of a temporary nature (e.g., boats, cars, people, football) are worshipped and then fail to satisfy, people often turn to Satan's next loop of temporary satisfaction. From boats, they might turn to cars, and then from cars they might turn to personal relationships. Then, from personal relationships they might turn on to buying houses. Thus, people can be deluded endlessly by Satan into thinking that this world can give them a sense of satisfaction, if they just keep pursuing it. This is Satan's great deceit. The restless human heart cannot be satisfied by anything except the supernatural saving grace of Jesus Christ. Because some people put their possessions and other people on a pedestal, they will eventually become disappointed when something about their perfection becomes imperfect. A person you admire suddenly has a personality flaw; a simple scratch on a new car sends someone into a fury. Eventually, these disappointments caused by Satan create a need for more and different things, which will become even greater and greater disappointments. Satan loves this type of illusionary control. Every time someone becomes obsessed with an earthly thing, Satan makes something happen to it. Then the person becomes obsessed with another earthly thing and something happens to it. Thus, the cyclic nature of sinful pursuit continues as people search for perfect happiness in an imperfect world.

Satan, of course, doesn't want you to be happy; he just wants to give you the temporary illusion of being happy. If Satan can string you along long enough—sometimes for an entire lifetime—then he can prevent you from asking a more important question: Where is all this buying and selling of temporary emotional fulfillment getting me? And the answer is: nowhere. Furthermore, Satan is distracting you from asking the most important question of your life: Where can I find permanent happiness? And, the only answer to this question is by turning towards Jesus Christ for forgiveness of your sins and by admitting to Him that you are a sinner and in need of His help for your salvation. If you turn towards Jesus, He will open a new spiritual door in your heart where you will see the foolishness of this world's idolatrous ways in favor of an eternal friendship with Him. Your relationship with Jesus Christ is the most important thing in your life because it leads to salvation and extends to life beyond this world and into the next. No other earthly thing can travel into the afterlife with you. The only earthly possession that you can take with you when you die is the love and the salvation offered to you through Jesus Christ. When you have come to know this noble and universal truth and have opened your hardened heart to Him, He will speak to you through your Holy Spirit and you will repent from your sinful ways.

Following Satan's whispers in your ear is a fruitless journey to unhappiness because worshipping anything other than Jesus Christ will prove to be a fatal mistake. "Lay not up for yourselves treasures upon the earth, where moth and rust doth corrupt (ruin), and where thieves break through and steal: But lay up for yourselves treasures in heaven, where neither moth nor rust doth corrupt (ruin), and where thieves do not break through nor steal" (Matthew:19-20). In the end, Jesus' love for you will provide you with a permanent and peaceful oasis from a fallen world fraught with psychological madness.

Questions
1. If the conditions are right, can we all act a little crazy at times? Explain one instance.
2. What earthly possession do you covet too much?
3. Why aren't earthly possessions found in heaven?

4. How does commercial television serve Satan's purpose?

My Story of Beowulf

Psalm 37:5 "Commit thy way unto the LORD; trust also in him; and he shall bring it to pass."

Theme: Talk is Cheap

One of my favorite pieces of literature is Beowulf an Old English epic poem about the shallow promise and support found in other people. Poems like Beowulf -- and other classic pieces of literature -- are read throughout the centuries because they provide a universal truth about human nature. Over the centuries the plot and characters in Beowulf have changed, depending on the century and on the country of origin. In fact, many versions of the story have surfaced around the world over the centuries, and I would like to add one more with the following.

The opening scene of the story is a Great Hall in Scandinavia with two blazing fireplaces at each end; large wooden beams frame the Great Hall's high ceiling, and a long crude wooden table in the center of the room stretches its entire length. Forty Viking men are sitting at the table, and they are dressed in crude animal fur. It's late at night, the fireplaces are blazing, and the men have spent the night drinking mead (strong beer). As the night gets older, and the Viking men drink more mead, they become emboldened and their boisterous conversation turns to confronting the dragon that lives in the lake below the hill near the village. Lately, the dragon has been coming up from the lake to the village and stealing woman and children. Although the dragon is large and scary, the more the men drink, the more they become convinced that they can go down to the lake and kill it. But just as their drunken confidence reaches a fervor pitch, the dragon shows up, kicks opened the barred door, and makes mayhem of their evening by killing some men and by making kindling of the Great Room.

The following evening, the Great Room scene is the same: fireplaces aglow, the beer a flow, and their voices a boasting about going down to the lake to kill the dragon. But on this evening, they discuss a plan for the next morning and appoint

Beowulf to lead them. Beowulf, convinced that they are committed to the task, accepts their appointment.

On the next morning, the men armed themselves with swords and spears and set out for the lake to slay the dragon. While walking to the lake with Beowulf in front leading them, their shouts of revelry about their impending victory spark confidence in everyone. That is, until they reach the lake's shoreline to confront the dragon, and Beowulf looks behind him and finds that the other fervent supporters are gone. Along their walk to the lake, they have had second thoughts about doing battle with the dragon, and they have abandoned Beowulf one-by-one and taken refuge by hiding behind trees in a forest near the lake. And now, Beowulf is standing alone at the shore to do battle with the dragon. When the dragon suddenly breaks the surface of the water from the depths of the lake, Beowulf does battle, and to make a long story short, Beowulf slays the dragon by himself to win the day.

Of course, this story's relevance and focus throughout the ages has been on the flaw in human nature to say one thing and do another. The braggards who talked a good game about helping Beowulf defeat the dragon, yet hid behind the trees, are still around today. Talk is still cheap, no matter the century. The lesson learned in Beowulf about human nature reminds me of those characters in the Bible who were fervent supporters of Jesus until they asked Jesus for advice on what they should do. In the case of the rich man, Jesus tells him to give away his vast possessions to the poor. And because the man had to make a sacrifice himself, he couldn't follow through. Jesus said to him, "If thou wilt be perfect, go and sell that thou hast, and give it to the poor, and then shall have treasure in heaven, and come and follow me. But when the young man heard that saying, he went away sorrowful..." (Matthew 19:21).

Jesus, of course, advised this process to the rich man because He knew that the rich man had many possessions that he worshipped as idols and that he wouldn't be able to give them up. It is a total commitment that Jesus seeks from us. Jesus doesn't want part-time Christians who put on a mask of piety on Sunday and talk a good game. He wants 24/7 Christians who will do what it takes to spread the Gospel.

However, when you're far away from Jesus, you cannot communicate with Him as well. It would be like those men centuries ago who hid behind the trees in the forest instead of standing alongside Beowulf at the lake. Their shouts of encouragement from afar didn't help much.

Questions
1. Think of a person who you cannot count on for support. Give an example.
2. What percentage of the time do you keep your word?
3. Who counts on you to keep your word?
4. What would happen to your well-being if Jesus did not keep His word?

The Easter Debt

1 Corinthians 13:11 "When I was a child, I spake as a child, I understood as a child, I thought as a child: but when I became a man, I put away childish things."

Theme: Our Debt to God

Looking back on it now, I now realize how innocently distorted my first Easter Sunday experience had been. As a child, I had quite a vivid imagination and an uncanny ability to draw my own conclusions. Unfortunately, my logic and the logic of the adult world often differed, which caused conflicting points of view.

It was four weeks before Easter in 1955, when my mother sat me in my father's favorite chair, an otherwise forbidden place, and said, "Stevie, your father and I have a favor to ask—we'd like to take tap dancing lessons." Naturally, because they were my parents, I agreed to take them, but it wasn't until starting that I learned why I was asked. It seems that the tap dance instructor owed my father some money and this was the only way she could repay it. Consequently, two lessons later I was abruptly jerked out of class because the debt had been paid.

A few weeks later after the tap-dancing episode, I was again sat in my father's favorite chair, but this time they wanted me to attend church on Easter Sunday. Because they had used the same method to persuade me, I logically concluded that God must owe my dad money too.

So, on Easter Sunday, I arrived at church and took a front row seat. However, it wasn't long after being seated that a huge man in a black suit told me to move to the back of the church. He said they needed room up front for the special Easter service. So, I moved to the rear of the church and found a seat near the clock; I suddenly remembered my dad was picking me up at noon.

For the most part, the East service was confusing, especially the part when they dunked a kinky-haired girl head-first into a bucket of water. The time did pass quickly, however. And before long I soon found it was two minutes before noon, so with the pastor still talking to the kinky-haired girl, I slipped out of my seat and headed for the backdoor. But when I reached it, the huge man in the black suit was standing there. "Where do you think you're going?" he asked.

"Outside to meet my dad," I replied. "It's noon."

"Didn't you know that on Easter Sunday that we have a longer service?"

"No, I didn't," I replied, still heading for the door. "But if the Lord wants to take more than one payment off his debt for the longer service, tell Him that He'll have to talk to my dad."

Questions
1. Describe an incident in your childhood where your conclusion was false.
2. Experience in life helps us to make better decisions. Explain one great decision that you made early in life with just enough experience.
3. It's true that some people never grow up. List some of their personality traits.
4. 1 Corinthians 13:11 states that we are to put away childish things. Name some childish things that you have put away.

The Library's Silo

Psalm 27:1 "The Lord is my light and my salvation: whom shall I fear?"

Theme: Life's Unpredictable Perils

In middle school no one wanted to be caught in the library during a fire drill because of the frightening prospect of using "the chute," a nickname given to the fire escape silo. The fire escape silo was a 5-story steel tube with a circular slide inside so that students could use it as a fire escape. The silo didn't have interior lights, so you had to essentially slide downward in a 5-story circle in the darkness of a steel tube. And no one wanted the responsibility of being the first student down the chute to open the steel door at the bottom because locating the door latch in the dark was a nightmare. Of course, there were always those mischievous students who wanted to be the first student down the chute so that they could create mayhem by not opening the exit door at the bottom. If this happened, then screaming students would stack up behind them on the slide in the darkness of the five-story steel tube. This scenario happened to me once; I got stuck in the middle of the dark silo with students piling up on the slide behind me. Their screams were deafening.

How you exited the silo's exit door at the bottom was also uncertain, although the construction concept was that everybody would smoothly exit the silo by landing gracefully on their own two feet. This graceful exit myth was further reinforced by the concrete slab located directly under the silo's exit door. As you might imagine, students fell out of the bottom of the chute at the exit door in an array of positions. Girls didn't want to use the silo's slide when they were wearing a dress. You can imagine the audience of teenagers standing on the concrete slab at the bottom of the chute applauding the various student landings.

When I tell this story, most people are horrified to think that this fire escape slide even existed. However, being trapped inside the darkness of a steel silo for what seemed like a lifetime is not so uncommon. Many people experience the same terror every day when their life slowly slides down in a spiral and they don't know how to escape it. For family and friends outside the silo, their life seems great. However, when you are inside and alone in the darkness of your own silo, it is terrifying. The downward slide is accompanied by feelings of apprehension and anxiety because life is so unpredictable. And even when family and friends offer comfort and support, it is often not enough, and the gloom of downward uncertainty continues.

However, there is good news for those anxious people who fear their own unpredictable future; they do not have to slide down their future alone because they have Jesus Christ as their own personal friend and Savior. He is unique because He is always close, He will never forsake you, and He can see your future and shine a light into it. All you need to do is to talk to Him through prayer. In fact, Jesus Christ's mission during His life on earth was to heal your heart and your fears. He died for you so that you could live your worldly life unafraid. If you haven't prayed to Jesus about your personal salvation and if you haven't read His Word in the Bible, now is the time because you're missing out on a life-transforming experience. If you pray to Him, Jesus will take you out of the darkness of life in your own personal downward slide and gracefully exit you into the brightness of His saving light.

Questions
1. Before you came to know Jesus Christ, did you often feel alone and in the dark? Explain.
2. At the time, why couldn't friends and family help you?
3. What was your first clue that Jesus was entering your life?
4. What were you afraid of before you met Jesus Christ?

Being Mugged on Halloween

2 Corinthians 11:26 "…in perils of robbers…."

Theme: The Dynamics of Good and Bad

When I was 8 years old, my parents let me trick-or-treat with a school friend if we stayed within two blocks of my house. I could tell that my parents were reluctant to let me trick-or-treat without them, but I pleaded with them and they finally consented. It's dark and spooky in Michigan in late October, and my friend and I walked close together on the sidewalk as we traversed from house to house. Finally, we finished with all the houses in our two-block radius, and we were just walking up to the backyard of my own house when suddenly some big kids ran out from the shadows of a neighbor's house, knocked me down, and stole my bag of candy. My friend was bigger and outran them to my back porch, but I was the victim of being mugged for my candy on Halloween. When I told my parents, my father—a burly, WWII ex-Navy vet, prowled through the neighborhood streets looking for them. For some reason, I was glad that he didn't find them.

When we returned to our house, my dad telephoned my grandmother to tell her about what had happened to me, and she insisted that we come over to her house so that she could replenish my candy bag. When we arrived at her house, grandma gave me a big hug and then started filling my candy bag with fruit. Apples, oranges, pears, and eventually a grapefruit plopped with a thud into the bottom of my brown grocery bag. Apparently, my grandmother had run out of Halloween candy herself, so she had retrieved what she could acquire from around the house. At the time, while I was grateful for my grandmother trying to make up the difference for my stolen Halloween candy, a boy of eight years most often will choose a Snickers Candy Bar over an apple any day. Nonetheless, I was grateful, and I thanked my grandma and we left. When my father and I returned home, my older brother had returned from his own trick-or-treating. And, of course, his bag was almost full of truly great treats. After my parents pleaded with him, he consented to take me down the street to a couple of houses to trick-or-treat to get some candy on Halloween.

So, we walked and stopped by a few houses for my benefit, and then at one house we were strangely invited to come inside and to sit down on the living room sofa. We were still wearing our masks, and the elderly couple kept looking at each other and winking, as if they knew something. Then, the woman stood up, went to the kitchen, and brought back two large bags of candy especially prepared for someone. She presented us with the bags of candy and then told us to take off our masks, as if to say the game was over. My brother and I took off our masks, and suddenly they became aware that we were not who they thought we were, but total strangers. Total strangers were now sitting on a sofa in their living room. Our costumes and masks had fooled them, and now I had a big bag of candy to show for it. That is, until the woman jerked the specially prepared bags of candy from our hands and told us to get out!

So, that year on Halloween I was mugged twice in one night. One time I was mugged in the darkness where the evil took place, and another time I was mugged of my candy in a brightly lighted living room. Even today, I am happy that our costumes had fooled those people. After all, isn't that the reason in the first place for wearing a Halloween costume? But at the same time, I was saddened by the woman taking back my candy; I had won it fair and square. Yet, still today somewhere deep down inside my Christian heart, I feel worse for the big kids who had to lurk in the darkness, jump out of the shadows, and push an innocent little boy to the ground to steal from him.

Unfortunately, my Halloween story was not over. The next morning on a Saturday, I went at 9:00 am to my elementary school gym to play dodgeball. My elementary school hired a high school student for a couple of hours on Saturday morning to supervise kids while they played in the gym. Usually, I never recognized the high schooler doing the supervision, but on this Saturday, I did. I recognized him because of his brown leather jacket; it was worn on the previous night by one of the big kids who had jumped out of the shadows and robbed me of my Halloween candy. How could it be the same kid? Last night he was a thug and a thief, and this morning he was laughing and supervising our play at the gym. How could he be both a good and a bad person?

Questions
1. What kind of masks do you wear throughout the day?
2. If sin exists in everyone because this is Satan's fallen world, how can we fight it?
3. Do most sins occur, even though those people doing it know that it is sinful? If so, then why does it happen?
4. Why does sinful behavior still happen, even among Christians?

Desert Places and Electronic Monkeys

Mark 1:40-45

Theme: Seeking Peace and Quiet

When Jesus withdrew to those desert places around Galilee because the cleansed leper had "blazed abroad the matter" (Mark:45) about the news of his cleansing by Jesus, even though Jesus had specifically told him not to say anything, the crowds of people who had come to see Jesus made it impossible for Him to be alone. So, he left to be alone in the desert with His Father God. In fact, desert places are necessary for all of us to renew ourselves spiritually so that we, too, can put the chaos of the world around us into perspective. It seems simple, at first—removing yourself physically from others to nurture the Holy Spirit. However, the clamor of today's outside world often follows us to our desert places so that the distractions continue, even though we have physically removed ourselves. Cell phones clang, satellite dishes serve up television commercials, and various other electronic devices clutter the landscape of our mind as we attempt to find solitude. Being off the grid has almost become a myth, for we often cannot escape to desert places in the globalized chatter of electronic communication.

Like mosquitos at dusk, the electronic hum swirls around us, and it seems that people no longer respect the dignity of quiet solitude. Our solitude has become their desert place, too, and they have brought their amplified music. God likes music too, and there are many references in both the *Old and New Testaments* about the musical accompaniment for celebrations and travel, and let's not forget about the trumpets at Jericho. Yet, music and noise, in general, had a place in the world back then. Boisterous celebrations were confined to the parameters of those revelers whose voices rose no further than other ears of people who could appreciate its loudness. Now, however, your noise is my noise in an amplified world, and no such dignity is afforded anyone who seeks the quiet of a desert place.

When was the last time you found total quiet without the

electronic dogs of the restless world barking at your presence? It's rare to find a physical space without sound. Right now, in my kitchen where I think that I'm alone, the refrigerator hums, the air-conditioner crackles, and the voices of people outside spoil the silence with intrusive regularity. "I hear it so much that I don't hear it anymore" is not the answer to finding the peace of a desert place. It is similar to the statement that "The place is so crowded that nobody goes there anymore." If nobody goes there, then how can the place be crowded? And if the solitude is broken by intrusive noise, how can a place be quiet? Some people, of course, don't want or need quiet; they couldn't recognize quiet on a sunny day at noon. They can't recognize it because they cannot see the inherent value of removing oneself from the screech of the world to become one individual person again.

When alone in their own thoughts and without the chatter of electronic monkeys, they may find that being alone with yourself is more difficult than most people think and removing oneself like Jesus to a desert place to be alone with God can be very scary. If you think about it, what do you say to the Creator of the Universe, especially if he's been waiting at your desert place to talk to you for your entire life? Do you say, I'm sorry about missing the point to my whole existence? How about, you plead the Fifth and ignorance and just say, "I didn't know." Whatever you say, God will hear it because He hears everything, even the beating of your heart. And, I guess that's the point. Finding a desert place where God awaits to talk to you is a heart issue; you simply have not opened your heart to hear His voice through the Holy Spirit to seek solitude within yourself and to refresh yourself in His Word. Your own desert place is the peace and solitude that you will find inside yourself when you seek God. He is in you, and the outside clamor can be escaped by finding that desert place within yourself where He awaits.

Questions
1. Where do you go to escape the clamor of the world to read the Bible to be with Jesus?
2. Do you know any Christians who have found the spiritual peace of a desert place within themselves?

What characteristics do you see in them?
3. Can prayer and the peaceful pursuit of being alone with God at the same time every day be helpful in finding a desert place?
4. What do you discuss with God when you're in your desert place?

The Charcoal Factory

John 16:33 "These things I have spoken unto you, that in me ye might have peace. In the world ye shall have tribulation: but be of good cheer; I have overcome the world."

Theme: Work and Tribulation

When I was in my junior year of college, I was forced by economic necessity to work full time from midnight to 8 am in a charcoal factory. The charcoal factory did not accept part-time workers, so anyone employed by it had to work full-time. Years later, the charcoal factory was closed by the EPA for environmental and health violations, but at the time when I worked there, it was a full-blown environmental nightmare. You could smell the charcoal chemistry for city blocks before you entered the factory's main gate. Once inside, the factory's property was a bleak, man-made hell of stench and darkness that stretched over a 10-acre area. The coal dust and the chemical process to make charcoal had left black pools of toxic waste over the entire area. The 10-acre site was surrounded by a 10-foot high chain-linked fence. I could never figure out whether the fence was there to keep people out or to keep people in.

I had two jobs at the charcoal plant: I either filled charcoal bags with charcoal bricks, or I joined three other workers to load an empty railroad boxcar by lifting 40lb charcoal bags. An eight-hour shift could produce 4 wooden pallets of newly filled and sewn charcoal bags, or on the railroad tracks an 8-hour shift was just enough time to fill one entire boxcar with 40lb individual bags. Both jobs were backbreaking and hazardous. For instance, the company's face mask didn't protect you when bagging charcoal, and the small charcoal bricks that free-fell from a chute on the ceiling into an awaiting empty charcoal bag would fill the surrounding air with charcoal dust every time the switch was activated. This resulted in the person doing the bagging to cough, wheeze, and gag. I blew charcoal dust from my nose routinely for months after I quit. I could also tell the men who had worked there for years; I could hear their deep cancerous cough long before I saw them. They were all walking cadavers, and they knew it.

While working at the charcoal factory from midnight to 8am, I was also attending college full time. I was carrying an academic load of 16 credit hours, four credit hours for four courses, including Shakespeare at 8:30am. I worked the midnight to 8am shift so there wasn't time to go home and shower before class, so I simply walked the one mile to my Shakespeare classroom. I was charcoal soot from head to toe, and when other students saw me looking for a seat in the classroom near them, they promptly scattered to other classroom spaces, as far away from me as possible. The Shakespeare instructor winced every time he saw me enter the classroom, and while we read Shakespeare — one of the most profound writers for understanding the human condition --- no one showed me any compassion. No one sat next to me; no one spoke to me; no one offered me any help socially or academically. I was alone in my own private hell. I looked like it; I smelled like it, and I coughed like it.

For months after I stopped working at the charcoal factory, the black charcoal dust could still be seen in the pores of my skin. My hands looked like they had never been washed. It was like the experience was so dark that I could never be washed clean. But one Memorial Day, I got a paid holiday off work, and I went to the beach on that sunny Memorial Day and reclined on my back on a sand dune and looked up at God's blue sky. I remember watching a silver jetliner far overhead, its speed and altitude creating a perfect white stream of vapor behind it. At the time, I wondered where the passengers on the airplane were going? What exotic destination awaited them? And, I wondered if God might cleanse me one day and allow me to soar upward like them?

Questions
1. Have you ever had a burden in life that you thought you couldn't bear?
2. What did it feel like when carrying those burdens alone?
3. Is that burden lessened by the love of Jesus Christ?
4. What do you pray when you ask Jesus to help you?

Snowstorm

Mark 4:39 "And he arose, and rebuked the wind, and said unto the sea, Peace be still: And the wind ceased, and there was a great calm."

Theme: The Types of Storms

    In 1966 when I was a freshman in college, I traveled home to see my parents for Thanksgiving. The trip was a 500-mile journey from Michigan's Upper Peninsula to where my parents lived in southern Michigan. The trip took eight hours to drive—first along the two-lane roads of the UP until the Mackinaw Bridge, and then south on I-75 on the four-lane through the length of Michigan's Lower Peninsula. In 1966 it was unseasonably warm for November, with the temperatures during the day in the high 60's to low 70's. So, I wore summer clothes home: a spring jacket, jeans, and penny loafers without socks. Thanksgiving with my parents that year was the first time that I had visited them since I had left home for college the previous August. It was a joyous reunion, one that featured the usual roast turkey, cranberries, and pumpkin pie, and my Thanksgiving visit went all too fast.

    When I left southern Michigan to return to college, the weather was still holding with usually high temperatures, and I anticipated the drive back with two college colleagues to be uneventful. However, about 4 hours into our drive and one hour south of the Mackinaw Bridge, we stopped for gas in Houghton Lake, and it was beginning to snow, and the warm comfortable temperature was rapidly declining. The 70-degree temps were now in the high 30's, and a gunpowder sky had replaced a blue one. In the gas station, people spoke of an impending blizzard beyond the Mackinaw Bridge to the north, and they warned us to be careful.

    By the time we reached the Mackinaw Bridge, the wind was howling, gusting to 55 mph, and blowing blizzard snowflakes sideways. On the UP side of the Bridge, Michigan State Police officers were stopping cars and huddling them together in groups and using both traffic lanes to go over the bridge. The groups of cars were going over side-by-side because it prevented the likelihood of any one car being blown off the Bridge.

When we reached the UP side of the Bridge and travelled west on US 2, we were the only car travelling on the road, and the road was covered in 15 inches of snow and navigating to stay on it had become difficult. Outside the car windows electrical lines alongside the road had snapped, and they were leaping and sparking from the telephone poles in the darkness. In a few minutes, the snow blowing off Lake Michigan had drifted up to the car's bumpers, and we had to plow through the deep snow at 15 mph. Even then, staying on the road was difficult. So, while one person drove, the other two passengers sat on the car's front fenders—one on each side—directing the driver by pointing at arm's length, left or right, as to how to stay on the road. A person could only sit on the car's front fender for about 20 minutes without going numb because of the cold. None of us had prepared for such a drastic shift in the weather, so our spring jackets weren't doing much good to keep out the cold. So, every 20 minutes we rotated positions: The person on the right fender went to the left fender, and the person on the left fender went inside to the warmth of car to drive, and the person driving went outside to sit on the right fender. Our routine went on like this for hours, with us traveling alone in a blizzard without seeing another soul. We became hopeful, however, after hours of isolation, darkness, and cold, when we saw a road sign that read "Marquette 12 miles." Northern Michigan University was in Marquette and we were almost home and back to the dormitory.

Then suddenly we drove upon a long line of cars stopped in the middle of the road; the taillights were barely visible in the furious wind and snow. What now? We all thought. We looked at our car's fuel gauge; it was just above one-quarter of a tank. If we set in our car for any protracted time, we would surely run out of gas. I got out of the car and walked up the long line of cars and knocked on car windows while seeking information. After talking to people in many cars, some with knowledge and some without, I returned to our car with the story. A semi-tractor trailer had jack-knifed across the road a few miles up ahead, but the police weren't going to tow it off the road until the weather broke and the blizzard stopped. With that information and the car's gasoline depleting, all three of us got out of the car, held hands to avoid being separated, and started walking in the blizzard along the long line of cars to find refuge. That night, we found a Greyhound bus driver who would let us stay on the bus for the night; there weren't any seats, but we could sleep on the bus floor in the aisle. When I awoke in the morning after sleeping on the bus floor, I saw the tread on the bottom of someone's snow boot one inch above my nose. I will never forget that image; it was like I was a bug that could be easily stepped on.

Fortunately, I had awakened before the person wearing the snow boots, and I found my friends and we exited the bus. We thanked the bus driver for his letting us onto the bus. His generosity probably saved our lives. Outside the bus, the dim light of a morning's dawn didn't help us to see; the blizzard snow and wind were still howling in a furry. We, again, walked by following the long line of cars, and eventually we reached a roadside tavern, which after nearly freezing to death was a welcomed sight. The name of the tavern was an appropriate one: The Idle Time. The bar was packed with about 250 travelers trying to sit out the storm. At first, the tavern's environment was friendly, warm, and cozy. However, when the first day led to the second day tempers of those huddled inside began to flare, partly because on the first day the tavern had run out of beer. The owner/bartender -- seeing a captive audience -- served anyone alcohol without checking an ID. Therefore, drinking was furious. So much so, that on the second day the wine and the booze also ran out. Then on the third day the toilets over-flowed and the furnace stopped. At that time, the situation became bleak, and the panic put into some personalities started to sound like that part in a horror movie when someone screams, "We're never going to get out of here!" I had not reached that point, but I was starting to wonder quietly about what was going to happen next? Then, on the morning of the fourth day, and after the blizzard had subsided leaving mountains of fluffy snow, a Michigan State Trooper showed up at the tavern's front door and announced that a tow truck had finally removed the jack-knifed semi-tractor trailer from the road and that cars were once again starting to move. We walked back to our car; it was about one-half mile from the tavern, and luckily our car's engine roared and we slowly followed the long line of cars the remaining 12-mile distance into Marquette.

In the dormitory, I looked in the bathroom mirror and saw that I had a good start on growing a beard, but my adventurous ways had waned by then, so I shaved. That afternoon, I heard on the radio that the blizzard had been the worst in 25 years in Michigan's Upper Peninsula and that people had been killed by it. Not far from the tavern where I had taken shelter, three people, while attempting to find shelter, had been found frozen to a tree, and numerous other deaths were attributed to heart attacks and hypothermia.

A few days after I had survived the blizzard, I met a girl in a nearby dormitory who had been stranded in the same tavern and had survived the storm. Because she was good looking and we had something in common, I was often seen hanging around her dormitory lobby on the off-chance that I might run into her and have a chance to strike-up a conversation. But when I finally got a chance to speak to her, I didn't even get a chance to offer up a lame one-liner like: "Didn't we go to different high schools together?" Instead, she insisted on asking the first question. Her first question to me was: "Are you saved?" "Saved from what?" I asked. She then promptly said, "I can't date you because we would be unequally yoked!" She then whirled around and quickly walked away.

It wasn't until 40 years later when I read the phrase "unequally yoked" in the Bible, as it pertained to unsaved and the saved people being together, that I finally understood what she meant. Over the years, I have since admired her for knowing the Bible and Jesus at such a young age. It took me nearly a lifetime to understand and to experience Jesus' gift of salvation, and it was my wife, a good Christian woman, who mentored me and set me on my life's path to seek out through prayer and Bible scripture Jesus' sacrifice for me and the essential meaning of life. At first, we were, indeed, unequally yoked, but as a Christian she saw in me some hope of becoming closer to Jesus. She knew that spreading the gospel to save others is the calling and responsibility of every Christian.

The Bible often speaks about how Jesus can help us to survive the travails of this worldly life. Yet, many people do not seek His help. My story about the deadly blizzard reminds me of how helpless I felt against the brute forces of nature. Then, I read the account in Mark 4:39 about how easily Jesus had rebuffed the winds of a storm at sea when the disciples thought their ship would sink and kill them. With a single wave of His hand, Jesus quelled the fierce storm and then probably went right back to sleep on a pillow at the stern of the ship. In fact, some scholars may even interpret His comment "Oh yea of little faith" (Matthew 8:26)) as a rebuke of His disciples for awaking Him from a sound sleep for such a petty matter. The disciples, however, didn't see the storm as petty. To them, and their human worldly power, it was life-threatening. While walking in a human chain in that snowstorm from car to car to find shelter, I also thought that my life was in danger. However, at the time I had not come to know Jesus, and I relied on my own human efforts to survive. But as demonstrated by the ease with which Jesus ended the sea storm for the disciples, man's worldly powers are certainly no match for God's supernatural powers. In my frightening snow story, there were probably other Christians in that place of shelter (besides the girl) who rightfully thanked God for their survival, and it would be years later before I would get a chance to do that with this story. I supposed that if Jesus had wanted to stop that windswept, four-day blizzard, He could have waved His hand to stop it at any time—just like He had done for His disciples at sea. It would have been startling to see a winter blizzard's gunpowder sky instantly explode to admit a sunny one. Today, most meteorologists would have logged it as an unprecedented scientific weather event and consulted their barometric pressure gauges for an answer. But to a Christian, only one interpretation could explain why the storm started and then stopped so suddenly; it was the intervention of the Lord's supernatural hand. On the day that Jesus calmed the disciples' storm, the disciples were so confused by it that they did not have an answer, but only a question, "What manner of man is this, that even the wind and sea obey Him?" (Mark 4:41).

In conclusion, I was never certain about what kind of storm

was the most dangerous—the storm outside of us or the storm inside us? Of course, when you're in a storm of nature -- whether a hurricane, tornado, or typhoon -- you're always certain that this kind of man vs nature storm is the worst. However, lately I am beginning to think that our own personal psychological storms might be the worst because they last longer and are deadlier. Satan's influence in the world has created a whirlwind of psychological storms for us. Abortion, gun violence, human trafficking, pornography, and divorce are at the top of the list of psychological storms that need calming. Make no mistake: The psychological storms of human weakness are just as frightening and deadly as any hurricane. A psychological storm just doesn't blow in one minute at 160 mph and then blow out. The inner storms of a personal psychological nature often swirl within us for a lifetime.

Questions
1. Name one personal psychological storm that you are battling?
2. Have you asked Jesus to calm the storm by praying?
3. Has Jesus sent anyone to help you?
4. What was the origin of the storm?

Middle School Gangs

Psalm 119:66 "Teach me good discernment and knowledge, For I believe in Your commandments."

Theme: Discernment

A good day for me in middle school was a day when I didn't get physically assaulted. Middle schools can be a dangerous place just because of the hormone challenges faced by all children that age. But it is especially challenging when your middle school is a migratory route for students. Many of the students in my middle school were the children of Mexican migrant workers who picked grapefruit in Texas in the winter and then moved to Michigan for the remainder of the year to pick tomatoes or cherries. Hence, the children of these migratory workers spent most of their school years in different schools and in different states and struggling to get an education. Some succeeded in getting an education by graduating from high school, and a few went to college. But most of them did not because they became too discouraged about their migratory path in life, and they knew that they couldn't catch up academically; there just weren't enough hours in the day. So instead of studying they acted out their displeasure with anti-social behavior. Some didn't attend class and instead robbed lunch money from unsuspecting students who entered the restroom. Other malcontents formed gangs, beat up their classmates, and used drugs. Unfortunately, one Saturday morning after my 8th grade basketball practice, I found myself face-to-face and walking into the middle of the worst gang in school.

It happened so fast that I couldn't avoid it. I was walking towards home and they were walking towards me going to a bowling alley, and we both walked around a blind corner of a tall downtown building, and I walked right into them. There was no turning back. I couldn't run. They would catch me, beat me up, or worse, put me in an ambulance on its way to the hospital. I had no choice but to stop, stay calm, and start talking nonchalantly – as if I wasn't afraid of them. Although I was terrified inside, I tried my best to conceal it. "Where are you going?" I quickly asked nonchalantly, before they could think about beating me to a pulp. For a few moments, there was dead silence. Then one guy who knew me because he made me cheat on history tests by giving him answers, finally said "To the bowling alley." Suddenly, the gang of eight started moving and shifting collectively to the left and into the direction of the bowling alley and I was caught up in the middle of their movement and was moving with them; I didn't have a choice and they knew it. So, I was hijacked by them into walking with them for the next four city blocks to the bowling alley. They surrounded me so that I couldn't run, even if I wanted to. Right after they made their collective left turn, which now included me, I began to talk about bowling. I had been in a bowling league for a couple of years, so I knew something about it. "Are you going bowling?" I asked. "No," a voice responded somewhere behind me; we don't know how to bowl. We're going to shoot pool." "Speak for yourself," another voice said from somewhere. "You roll a ball and try to hit the front pin head-on." Of course, I knew that you didn't hit the front pin head-on; you tried to hit next to it, but I didn't say anything. I didn't want to contradict someone and possibly start a fight.

    For the next four city blocks, I asked question after question and let them talk about themselves. People like to talk about themselves, even middle school gang members. While I walked for four blocks in the middle of the eight gang members, I was seen by other students riding by in their parents' car and by students walking on the other side of the street. Four blocks later at the bowling alley, I made a plausible excuse to leave them, and they went into the bowling alley, and I ran home as fast as I could.

    To my surprise on Monday morning at middle school no one tried to bully me; the word had gotten out that I had been seen walking downtown on Saturday in the middle of the toughest gang in school. Even the bigger guys in metal shop class, who usually bullied me, never bothered me again. Years later, I heard from a classmate that the one gang member who had spoken to me first on that Saturday morning to start the conversation had enlisted in the Marines and had served three combat tours in Vietnam. Maybe while there, he had learned how to pray to God. Someone once said that there are no atheists in combat. Eventually, the former gang member turned Marine attended college on the GI Bill, earned a Ph.D. in sociology, and taught college. The remainder of the gang members—all penitentiary bound—were never heard from again. But on that day when I accidently met that gang while walking around a blind corner of a city building, a 13-year-old kid scared out of his wits learned how to apply the gift of discernment given to him by God. It was a heavenly gift given to me by God at the right moment, and a gift that has remained with me for a lifetime.

Questions
1. What are some of your gifts given to you by God?
2. Name a situation when you have used one of those gifts?
3. When did you first learn of that gift from God?
4. Who else recognizes that gift in you?

Dracula

Psalm 25:7 "Remember not the sins of my youth, or my transgressions: according to thy mercy remember thou me for thy goodness' sake, O LORD."

Theme: Superficial Conclusions

I arrived late at my first day of Political Theory class because I had overslept. The class began at 9:00 am, and my alarm clock malfunctioned, so I was the last student to enter the college classroom. All the classroom seats had been taken, except the one seat in the front row at the center of the classroom. No one wanted to sit in the "hot seat," as it was named, because professors loved to call on the student who sat there because it was a convenient "go-to" location. Any professor who wanted to pretend to be asking the entire class a question -- but couldn't be bothered -- pretended to ask the entire class a question by calling on the student who occupied the hot seat. The mission of the hot seat student was to answer the professor's numerous questions for the entire class. The questions weren't tough, but the hot seat student had to always pay attention to answer them correctly. If the hot seat student failed to answer a hot seat question correctly, the professor would grimace wildly at the hot seat student's incorrect answer, look at the other students, as if to say, that the hot seat student was a loser, and then roll his eyes and answer the question himself. Therefore, the hot seat student had to attend class every day; his absence would be conspicuous, and he had to be prepared to answer the questions correctly.

Unfortunately, because of my late arrival on the first day of class in Political Theory, the "hot seat" was mine. And once a seat is occupied on the first day of class, it is that student's seat in the classroom for the remainder of the semester. It is an unwritten law in college classroom etiquette. The seat taken on the first day of class officially becomes yours and stakes your classroom claim to the territory. Therefore, I was the occupier of the classroom hot seat for the entire semester. I knew it, and everyone else in the classroom did too.

My tenure as the hot seat occupant, however, was short lived. In fact, my occupancy lasted less than 5 minutes because I dropped the class. As soon as the professor appeared at the door, I wanted to leave because he scared me. He was middle-aged and gaunt, wore a black suit, white dress shirt, and skinny black tie; he had long, jet black hair that was slicked back on the sides with the oiliness of 10W40 motor oil. His face was pasty white, narrow, and drawn inward at the cheek bones, which made his pointed nose look even longer. After setting his lecture notes down on the wooden podium in the front of the classroom, he looked up directly at me in the hot seat with his piercing black eyes and said, "Goot Mournink" in a severe Transylvanian accent. He apologized for his accent and stated that he had only recently arrived in the United States after booking passage on a cargo freighter from Europe. Suddenly, I knew that he had not travelled first class but that he had travelled in the ship's cargo hold in a wooden coffin half-filled with native Transylvanian soil. That's right! I dropped a college class because I thought the professor was Dracula.

Over the years, I have learned that appearances can be deceiving. In fact, now that I am living in my Christian skin, I wish it was easier for me to recognize other Christians. During the Crusades knights wore white robes emblazoned with red crosses; perhaps it would be easier to recognize a Christian today if we all dressed the same. However, even if we all worn white robes with red crosses, it wouldn't necessarily denote the good guys from the bad. Today, many nonbelievers dress in heavy Christian gear, including huge crosses dangling around their neck. Likewise, Christian believers today don't have a distinctive look either. They could resemble Noah, complete with beard and wooden staff—or not. Or, they could just as easily ride a Harley, ride a tractor, or ride a surfboard to church on Sunday. God wants and needs people from all walks of life to fulfill His earthly ministry. Christians might all look different outwardly, but inwardly they all feel the same warmth in their heart by having a sincere love for the Lord Jesus Christ. Jesus has placed that love for Him in them since the foundation of the world so that the Holy Spirit could nurture their faith to receive His gift of salvation. Consequently, you can't identify Christians by appearance; but you can identify them by their similar love for Jesus.

Hebrews 13:2 states "Be not forgetful to entertain strangers: for thereby some have entertained angels unawares." This reiterates our Christian obligation to talk to strangers. Of course, Satan tells you to be afraid of strangers and to be reluctant to talk to them because Satan wants people to be isolated and wary of each other. In this way, he can control our lives and prevent Christians from getting the opportunity to bring another lost soul to Christ. If we do not have the courage to do what is right, then we must be doing what is wrong—which falls into Satan's temporary influence in this world.

Fifty years ago, as a naïve and imaginative 17-year-old college freshman who was terrified of his college professor, I wrongly dropped a political science professor's class based on my biased opinion about his appearance and cultural background. My imagination led me to leave his classroom and the political science program for the Creative Writing Program. Although it was eventually a good academic decision, it was a decision made for the wrong reasons. We can't judge people; that is God's academic department. No one Christian will resemble another in appearance, and no one Christian's personality will be identical to another. God made all Christians different, yet we all hear the same voice when He calls to us in our hearts. He expects us to do good in the world by being engaged with it and not by running from it. It is Satan telling us to fear each other, and it is just the opposite of God's message.

Questions
1. Explain one incident where you misjudged a person by their appearance.
2. Do adults dress differently for different occasions? Name some types of dress.
3. Explain one time when you made a bad impression because of your appearance.
4. Describe your favorite casual clothes. Do you have a favorite shirt, etc.?

My Cat Gets Arrested

Isaiah 28:16 "Behold, I lay in Sion a chief corner stone, elect, precious: and he that believeth on him shall not be confounded."

Theme: Trying to Rearrange God's World

    Many years ago, I lived in Marquette, Michigan on the shores of Lake Superior where the summers are a sweet relief from the brutal and long winters. It was on one of these sweet summer mornings that I received a knock at my front door. Upon answering the door, I saw two uniformed city police officers. At first, the police officers looked down nervously at their shoes and were reluctant to speak. Then, I thought the worst; a family member had been killed in a car accident; someone that I knew had fallen off a Lake Superior break wall and had drown. After seeing the panic slowly rising on my face, one of the officers spoke. He started the conversation by saying "That, by law, he was required to follow up on all complaints telephoned in to police headquarters. This morning police headquarters had received a telephone call from your neighbor complaining about your cat. The neighbor reported that your cat was chasing his birds." I replied, "If my cat is chasing his birds, then his birds must be chasing my worms."
    Every day, humans try to control and re-direct God's plan on earth. And every day, humans who try to grab the baton from God's hands to re-direct his world to get it to sing another song fail. Somewhere along their life's path, some people mistakenly received the wrong memo about their role on God's earth. People are not here to serve their own purpose; they are here to follow God's purpose for them. And while we often don't understand why something happens to us, we must always remember that God doesn't have to explain any of His actions to us. If God wants cats to chase birds, they will. And, if God wants birds to chase worms, they will. It is not for us to try and divert God's will to suit our own purpose. By doing so, we display our ignorance and arrogance that we know more than God in our attempts to "make things right."
    People who don't understand that God is in charge will

constantly confront other people in earthly situations about God's world because they don't read the Bible to understand how things work. "To everything there is a season, and a time to every purpose under the heaven:" (Ecclesiastes 3:1) If people continually dispute with God about His ordering of the universe, then they are out of their league. God doesn't create imperfection; just look around at the wonderful balance in nature with every species, plant, flower, and fauna doing exactly what God directs them to do. In fact, the only disobedient creature who steps out of bounds in his obligation to do the will of God is man.

Every fall season I watch the perfect V-winged flight of geese migrating south. Before they go on God's programed migration each year and follow God's will directing them, they don't call the city police to ask what to do; they know exactly what to do, and so does man. Yet, man doesn't rely on God's Word; he thinks that he knows more than God. It's kind of pathetic how humans try to slap God's hands away from His own creation. But then, if you don't know how it all works on earth because you don't read the Bible, then you're destined to migrate on your own merit towards a permanent southern trajectory.

Questions
1. What things in your life do you try to over-control?
2. How do you feel when your efforts fail?
3. When was man's disobedience to God first experienced?
4. Where is the permanent southern trajectory?

The Bulldozer

Acts 15:20 "But that we write unto them that they abstain from pollutions of idols...."

Theme: Wants and Needs

Some years ago, a member in my small church group was an engineer for John Deere, and it was his job to travel throughout the world trouble-shooting any problems with John Deere heavy equipment. Usually, his travels took him to various corporate headquarters to examine a piece of large machinery to assess its problem. But one time he found himself traveling on a gravel road up a West Virginia mountainside to visit a residential house where the owner was having a problem with his $375,000 bulldozer.

My engineer friend followed a circular gravel road all the way to the mountaintop, where the road suddenly ended at a residential driveway and a big house with a large pre-fabricated building next to it. My friend got out of his car, walked to the house, and knocked on its front door. The door was opened by a middle-aged man of about 50 years, and my friend introduced himself as the trouble-shooter sent by John Deere, whereupon my friend was led by the man over to the large pre-fab building where he slid open a wide door to reveal a new $375,000 bulldozer. My friend looked outside the door again and saw no sign of the bulldozer being used. No earth had been up-ended for miles. In fact, the house's yard was quite small. My friend went about examining the bulldozer because that was his job and why he had arrived, but when he had found the problem and ordered a new part over his cell phone, his curiosity got the best of him, and he just had to ask why an individual, and not a corporation, would own such a large and expensive piece of equipment and seemingly never use it? To which the man answered, "I won the Power Ball Lottery worth $150 million a few months ago, and I had always wanted my very own John Deere bulldozer."

Moderation has never been one of natural man's personality traits. The world is full of things, and natural man is in a candy store when it comes to buying them. However, this excessive consumerism is just the opposite of how Jesus instructed his disciples to prepare when He sent them forth into the world to spread the gospel. He instructed them to take no money, one pair of sandals, no change of clothing, and no food. In short, they carried only themselves into their mission for Christ. This approach certainly looks different from today's Mega-churches excessive use of carnival theatrics to spread the Word of God. How Jesus sent out His disciples into the world teaches us how to simply and humbly approach the learning and teaching of the Word of God. In fact, anytime you leave the Bible's page to employ some device, you also run the risk of usurping the Word's instruction in favor of that intruding device. Therefore, despite the showmanship of dry ice fog and the blinding flash of multi-colored strobe lights, many people who go to church still don't read the Bible. Why? Well, it's because they've become lost in the elaborate church pyrotechnics and are being entertained instead of being instructed.

Jesus didn't send His disciples into the world with bottle rockets to preach His gospel. He sent them out into the world alone with the Word of God and that's what God requires of us. Being alone with the Bible and absorbing God's Word is an active process that requires intimate participation, whereas being subjected to artificial church theatre creates a passive participant and disengagement. God doesn't need any carnival acts to bulldoze His message through the excesses of fallen world. He just needs your simple desire to get to know Him by reading His Word in the Bible.

Questions
1. Name some theatrics used by churches to keep their congregation's attention?
2. Is this use of theatre attracting or distracting people?
3. At what point does ritual become theater?
4. Do some religions rely more on theater than others? Name some.

How My First Dated Ended

John 6:1 "Children, obey your parents in the Lord: for this is right."

Theme: A Parent's Advice

    When I was a young man in junior high school, my parents had established a dating policy that I couldn't officially date until the 8th grade Christmas Dance. So, the 8th grade Christmas Dance was a big personal event for me. In addition, the Junior High Christmas Dance was also a big social event because it was the only formal dance of the entire school year where the guys wore sport coats and the girls wore formal gowns. What you wore to the dance and how you looked was extremely important. It was so important to me that I started trying on various clothing combinations two weeks prior to the dance. I had invited a young girl named Sandy Dee to the dance, and I wanted to look perfect. I was sure that she was trying on dresses to also look perfect. My dad had agreed to drive us to the dance after picking her up from her house. Yet, no mattered what combination of clothes I tried on in front of my bedroom mirror to wear to the dance, they all had one glaring error: my old shoes.
    No matter how much polish I put onto my old shoes, they simply didn't hold up to the scrutiny of wearing much nicer clothes. So, two weeks before the big dance, I started verbally working on my dad to buy me some new shoes. I figured that it would probably take at least two weeks to wear him down to give in to my new shoe demands. I started with subtle new shoe hints at first. Then, as the days progressed and drew nearer to the dance date, my suggestions about getting a new pair of shoes for the Christmas Dance turned into borderline badgering. Then, finally on late Friday afternoon on the night of the Christmas Dance, he agreed to go with me to the shoe store on Main Street. However, just before we left for the shoe store, he cautioned me that wearing slippery new shoes in winter would be like wearing a new pair of ice skates. The shoe's new and slick leather soles simply wouldn't provide any traction; every step I took would be a hazardous one. To make

matters worse, it started snowing on the afternoon of the dance. But I was determined to complete my clothes perfectly for the important Christmas Dance, so despite my dad's warning we left to buy me some new shoes.

By the time we arrived downtown to the Main Street Shoe Store, the snow was falling heavily and the wind was howling, but it didn't take me long to spot the perfect shoes through the shoe store's plate glass window. They were a pair of black leather loafers that perfectly matched my Christmas Dance attire, and we went inside the shoe store and bought them.

By 7:00 pm, the winter weather had reached blizzard pitch, yet after such elaborate preparations for the dance, I was determined to go, and so was my date Sandy Dee, who I had telephoned a few minutes before to confirm our date. I had never been to Sandy Dee's house; she lived on the other side of town and riding a bicycle for transportation limits a guy's access to women. So, when my dad pulled his car up to Sandy's house to pick her up for my date, I discovered that she lived in a house atop a steep hill. The house had 75 concrete steps leading up the hill to it, and an iron railing was alongside the steps for support. Yet, after leaving the warmth of my dad's car, I soon discovered that the steps were snow-covered and that the iron railing was coated with ice. In fact, the steps were about 95% snow-covered, and only a small two-inch portion at the front of each step remained uncovered. I made my way up the stairs by carefully placing each shoe directly onto the narrow, dry surface at the front of each step and by hanging onto the slippery iron railing and pulling my way up the stairs hand-over-fist.

When I finally reached the top of the 75 steps leading up the hill to Sandy's house, I discovered that the porch was also ice covered, slippery, and slanted forward from the house. Two porch columns supported the porch roof, so I shuffled my way up the slippery porch floor in my new shoes by clinging to a porch column to eventually reach a clear patch of floor near the house's front door. I looked in the house's front window, and Sandy's parents were taking photographs of her in front of the fireplace in the living room, and she was beautifully dressed in a dark blue prom gown. Her hair was piled high on her head in a beehive hairdo; it was the hair style of the time, and I supposed the bane of many low flying airplanes. When I saw that her parents had finished taking Sandy's photograph, I knocked on the front door. Her father answered the door, and suddenly I was inside feeling the welcomed warmth of their fireplace. After a few introductions and photographs of Sandy and me standing before the fireplace, we stepped outside onto the icy front porch to go down the steep front yard steps to reach my dad's parked car at the bottom of the hill. Thus far, the evening had gone as planned. I was wearing my perfect clothes -- complete with new shoes, and I had made it up Sandy's treacherous front yard steps to her house without falling in the icy winter conditions, and now all I had to do was accompany Sandy down the hill to my father's car where we would be whisked away to the dance.

I was thinking these wonderful thoughts when we stepped from Sandy's front porch onto the sidewalk leading to the concrete steps when Sandy's right foot suddenly slipped out from under her, and she grabbed onto my left arm to keep from falling. When she grabbed onto my left arm, it set me off-balance too, and both of my feet in my new shoes slipped out from under me, and I instinctively reached over to grab her to keep from falling. As a result, her left foot also slipped out from under her, and in a flash of a moment we were both falling to the ground and rolling down the hill in front of her house. We tumbled head-over-heels together down the hill, while still clinging to each another. Sandy's beehive hairdo was flopping and unraveling in long and uneven strands that slapped against the sides of her head, and her prom dress went flying up and over her head as we somersaulted our way down to the bottom of the hill where our tumbling stopped abruptly next to my dad's car. I remember my dad calmly leaning over from the driver's side to roll down the passenger's side window. Once the passenger's side window was rolled down, he looked at me and Sandy in our snowbound heap and simply said, "Nice Shoes."

Of course, that first dance in junior high school was almost a lifetime ago, and since then Jesus has two-stepped my life through a series of Christian changes. With Him by my side, I no longer care about how I appear by wearing the latest fashions. Wearing the latest clothing has ceased to be a life's priority. I am, however, well bathed; I'm sure Jesus likes me to be, but new shoes for special occasions no longer adorn my feet. Over the years, I have discovered that the latest clothing fashions are just a way to make money for other people and that old clothes—if they are cared for—seem to accomplish the same task of covering my physical self. Additionally, we are not what we wear; we are who we are by the touching of Jesus' hand. If clothes were that important to our spiritual well-being, we would all be born wearing Gucci this or Gucci that, yet instead of clothes adorning our body at birth, God humbles the miracle of birth by exposing us naked and afraid to the world. He does this so we know that God is the most important entity in our life until we slip into our last dance on earth to be with Him in heaven.

Questions
1. Describe a time when you ignored your parents' advice and got into trouble.
2. What does Jesus say about trouble in this world?
3. What does the Bible promise when you show respect and honor your parents?
4. When you needed money as a teenager, who did you ask your mom or your dad? Why?

Math and Science Class

Matthew 24:4 "Take heed that no man deceive you."

Theme: Complete What You Start

When I was a freshman in college, I was required to take a Math and Natural Science Class. Every freshmen student was required to take it, and because the freshmen enrollment had tripled at the university to include thousands of new freshmen students, it meant that every Math and Science class enrollment was huge. My Math and Science class had approximately 700 students, and because of its large enrollment the class was held in a huge lecture hall. In addition, the class was at 8:00 am, and it didn't take long for me to figure out that as a dormitory night owl that having an 8:00 am class was not a good thing. The lecture hall was also about one mile from my dormitory, so in rainy and snowy weather with the temperature near zero, I had to get up early and trudge a mile through inclement weather to get to class. Furthermore, because of the large class enrollment, no one instructor could handle the class size. Therefore, instead of one professor teaching at the front of the classroom, the university had installed a bank of 15 televisions on the classroom's walls to broadcast a video of a professor giving a lecture. Because an instructor was not present in the classroom, any student with a question had to write it on a slip of paper and drop it into a large wooden question box at the front of the classroom. At first, students with questions about the video lecture routinely dropped their slips of paper into the question box. However, when it became apparent after a few weeks that no questions were being answered, students stopped placing questions into the box. Although a tag on the front of the box stated that all questions would be answered within 24 hours, to my knowledge no questions were ever answered, including the eleven questions that I had personally dropped into the box.

Therefore, as television monitors droned complicated mathematical and scientific information about conditional and bi-conditional clauses related to scientific research, the enrollment after six weeks had plummeted to only a handful of nerds who probably should have tested out of the class in the first place. With all these format defects going for the class, I stopped attending in the fifth week because it was inconvenient and I was learning absolutely nothing.

Not going to class was great for a while. I could sleep in until 10:00am, and I could concentrate and use my time to study for my other three classes. Admittedly, for weeks I didn't even think about the Math and Science class, and many other students didn't either. That is, until the semester marched slowly forward to the final exam. The final exam for the Math and Science Class was recorded and scored electronically. On exam day, an unknown professor passed out the exam booklet, an electronic pencil, and an electronic score card on which to mark your answers. There were 350 questions and four blank spaces to mark one for each question. You know the drill, darken the space provided for in A, B, C, or D. On one hand, I was lucky because the final exam was being given electronically, so I could guess at an answer or just randomly mark down an answer. The exam was supposed to take 2.5 hours. However, after about the fifth question, I realized that I knew absolutely nothing, and I started to mark all the questions randomly by choosing the letter D. A final exam that was supposed to take me 2.5 hours, I finished in 10 minutes. I remember feeling kind of sheepish about finishing so quickly, so I just sat at my desk for a few minutes to at least make it look like I knew something. But then, I got bored, stood up, handed in my answer score card, and headed out the classroom door.

The next two weeks were agonizing. In those days, the college sent your final grades for all your classes by snail mail to your home address. I had been home for semester break for about two weeks, waiting for my final grades to arrive via US Mail. I knew that I had done well in my other three classes; not attending the Math and Science Class had freed up my time to concentrate on them. But the Math and Science Class final grade was a potential GPA nightmare. If the Math and Science grade was an F or a D, it would severely damage my overall GPA for the semester. Furthermore, if I failed the class I would have to take it again the following semester.

I had been checking the mailbox at my parents' house every day for nearly two weeks. Then the official grade transcript for the semester arrived. I remember holding the college envelope containing the grades in my hand and being afraid to open it. I remember even holding the envelope up to the sunlight in hopes of getting a sneak peek. Then, with a heavy heart I opened the envelop and looked at the grades inside: Math and Natural Science Grade: B. Of course, it would have been better to have studied and learned something from the class to earn and deserve a grade of B. Yet, at the time I felt a tremendous relief, even if the grade did not reflect my earned knowledge. To me, at that moment in time, it became all a number's game. It wasn't what I knew that counted; it was what I appeared to know. In fact, years later I would learn that deceiving others into thinking that you know something exists throughout the employment world; millions of people go to work every day and pretend that they are knowledgeable about their job, although they are out of their employment depth. "Fake it until you make it" is a popular phrase; it implies that being dishonest will eventually pay dividends if you can be deceitful long enough.

Not long ago, a friend of mine was being prepped to undergo heart surgery, and I told him this same Math and Science story to lift his spirits. Unfortunately, it did just the opposite. "Let's hope," my friend replied, "that the heart surgeon operating on me this morning didn't skip out of his heart valve replacement class because it was too early, too far to walk, or because he didn't like the format."

Now that I look back at my friend's comments and at the Math and Science story, the excuses to avoid my obligation to attend Math and Science class were many. Excuses abound in Satin's world, where absence and lies often prevail. Not doing what is morally right and ducking responsibility in the world has risen to a new level of escapism. Many people don't work at their jobs; they escape through the workday without working, drawing paycheck after paycheck without involvement or the requisite knowledge. Aloof from their work role, they help no one. Fortunately, God directed me away from a Math and Science career and into a creative writing one. He took me by the hand and led me into a career that was better suited to satisfy my spirit. In it, I don't duck responsibility; I embrace it as a friend given to me by Jesus. I am a better writer because of Jesus' help, and I believe that He reads every word that I write over my shoulder, as I try to write every word to His Glory. It isn't an easy job spreading the Gospel and bringing new Christians to Jesus; just ask the disciples. Yet, In the end, I hope He likes what I write enough to say at the end of my life "Well done good and faithful servant."

Questions
1. Do you know someone at work who is a fake at their job? Give some examples.
2. What would Jesus say about their job deception?
3. How do people get promoted to management positions when they don't even know what their subordinates do?
4. Is it Christian for a person to defraud an employer, even if he can get away with it?

Almost A Millionaire

Psalm 37:3 "Trust in the Lord, and do good; so shalt thou dwell in the land, and verily thou shalt be fed."

Theme: Trust in the Lord

When I was a young college professor teaching at a small college, I never made enough money teaching to survive. In fact, my college teaching salary was about $5,000 below the poverty level. So, during the summer months when the college was closed from May to September, I had to find summer work. Of course, I would have preferred to stay home and write, but my dire economic condition forced me into summer employment. I always had dreams of landing the perfect summer job—one that paid me a lot of money. But that perfect job never showed up, so I had to opt for any job that I could find. Usually, it was some form of manual labor. Then, one summer a once-in-a-lifetime job opportunity presented itself, but I was too blind to see it.

Near the end of one academic year, I was approached by a colleague in the English Department to edit his book manuscript. He said that he didn't have any money to pay me for my editorial work, but that he would pay me 1% to 2% of the royalties once he found a publisher. He said that he would get a lawyer to draw up a contract to that effect. At the time, I was poor and needed an immediate paycheck. This financial fact prompted my decision to take a summer job driving a dump truck. The truck driving job paid $4.85 per hour and it included a lot of overtime pay. The wage of $4.85 per hour was good money back then; the minimum wage was about $2.15 per hour, so I took the job. Otherwise, I could have spent hundreds of hours over the summer editing a book manuscript that might never get published.

Out of courtesy, I tried to decline editing my colleague's book gracefully, although he really didn't want to take "no" for an answer. The next day he brought his manuscript to my office for me to read. The manuscript was huge. When he set it down on my office desk, the 8.5 x 11-inch pages must have been piled in a stack two-feet high. When he left my office, I took a few pages off the top of the manuscript and began to read. John Cheever, the novelist, once said that writing is not a competitive sport. Yet, most writers like to compare their writing style with other writers, and I was no different. Upon reading a dozen or so pages, I discovered that my colleague had written a fantastic tale that would be a joy to read, but maybe a nightmare to edit. His prose style was dense with long, complicated sentences and editing it would, indeed, take the entire summer, so I politely declined.

A few weeks later, I learned that my English Department colleague had taken a teaching job at another college, so I thought that I would never see him again. Twenty-five years later, however, I did meet my colleague again. Well, we sort of met again. One day, I sat down in my living room to watch an HBO movie and his manuscript had not only been published, but it had also been made into a movie series. His book—the book that I had declined to edit-- had become a worldwide phenomenon and had sold millions of copies. If I had spent that summer editing his book instead of driving a dump truck, my 1% to 2% royalty contract would have been worth millions.

I wish that I had known the Lord Jesus back then. I would have prayed to Him about what to do. Win, lose, or draw, the events of life always seem to go easier with Jesus involved. If I had relied on Jesus to make that decision, the outcome might have gone differently, although the eventual outcome isn't the point. The point is the importance of including Jesus in any decision-making process – big or small. Instead of relying on myself, I could have relied on Him for direction. Jesus' supernatural advice is always a good thing to have, and His input should always be sought, no matter the outcome.

Questions
1. Relate a circumstance where something great almost happened to you.
2. How did a short-term failure eventually help you in the long-term?
3. God's plans for us and our plans for ourselves often don't coincide. Why are His plans always better, although they may not seem so at the time?

4. Why shouldn't we compare our life to someone else's life?

A Laughing Hyena

John 8:32 "And ye shall know the truth, and the truth shall make you free."

Theme: Finding the Truth

When I was in kindergarten, a vinyl record was played of wild animal jungle sounds by the teacher. The record contained the sounds made by elephants, monkeys, lions, etc. But the most distinctive sound was the high-pitched noise made by the hyena. It sounded like a person laughing hysterically. Of course, the sound made by the hyena was by far the most popular one of all my twenty classmates.

The first time that I heard the recorded sound of the hyena, I laughed, too. Then the following week when the record of the sound of the hyena was played again, I chuckled because it was only somewhat funny. The same record of the animal sounds was played once a week for eight weeks, and to my amazement each successive week that it was played to the other class members the hyena sound appeared to be as funny as when it was played the first time. By the third time that the hyena recording was played, I no longer thought that it was funny and didn't laugh. The teacher noticed that I was no longer laughing at the sound of the hyena and she asked me why? At first, I told her that I didn't know why, and then finally I confessed that I wasn't laughing because I had heard it too many times, whereupon she picked up a notebook from her desk and made some notes about me in it.

In the first grade, I was asked to draw a picture of my family members and the house where we lived. I drew a picture with various colors of crayon. I made my dad the tallest person in my picture, my brother the second tallest, and then my mother the shortest person in my picture. My family members were all lined up and standing next to each other in front of our house, which I colored with a black crayon.

A few days after my drawing was submitted to my first-grade teacher, I was taken out of class every Wednesday at 10:00 am to walk up a long flight of stairs to an office to talk to a woman. At the time, of course, I didn't know that the woman was the school district's psychologist. My meetings with the woman up the flight of stairs had gone on for eight weeks, when my mother asked me one day what I had done in school. It was on a Wednesday afternoon, so I told her about my long walk up the flight of stairs to talk to a lady. When I told her, she asked me, "How long have you been talking to the lady up the flight of stairs?" I replied, "weeks."

When my mom found out that I had been talking to the school psychologist for weeks without her permission, she went ballistic, and she trudged down to the school to find out why? The elementary school principal and the psychologist showed my mom the picture of the family members that I had drawn in crayon.

"So?" my mother asked.

"Well, your son has drawn a picture of your family members with his brother taller than you, which means that he must respect his older brother more than you. And that means that he has a general disregard for authority."

"Well," my mother replied, "my eldest son is actually taller than me, although he's only in the fifth grade."

"Well then," the principal continued, "that may well be true, but look at the black color he used to color your house."

"Our house is black, or at least a darker shade of gray. I bet my son's crayon box didn't have a gray crayon in it, so he chose to use black—the closest color to it."

"Well then, "the principal continued. "Last year in kindergarten he stopped laughing at the hyena sound on the animal record weeks before the other kids."

"That's because we often take him to the zoo, and he has heard the hyena sound a million times."

I never knew what was going on when my mother—quite steamed—abruptly visited my elementary school principal and the school district's psychologist about my visits up the long flight of stairs. However, five years later when I had won a writing award in the sixth grade for an essay about George Washington, I heard the principal say to my mom,

"See, I knew that together we could get him turned around."

Today, many people like to take credit when no credit is due. They like to take credit for solving a problem when no problem exists. As time lapses from an incident, the participants often re-create history in their favor. Despite the school's principal and the school district's psychologist's inaccurate assumptions about me, when confronted about them by my mother they probably still recorded in my personnel file that my conversations with the school psychologist had healed me, when in fact no healing was necessary. Satan's world is full of people who can't own up to their mistakes and must blame others or concoct an alternative narrative to off-load the blame. Amid this common deceit, it makes finding out the truth very difficult. Perhaps the only place where there is undisputable truth is in the Bible. "I am the way, (and) the truth…."

Questions
1. Explain an incident when untruthful assumptions were made.
2. Recall an incident where someone did not own their mistake.
3. Explain an incident where years later someone had concocted an alternative story.
4. How long does it take to create an alternative story. Describe a time when it took place immediately.

Look for the Dust Bunnies

1 Corinthians 10:31 "Whatever you do, do it all for the glory of God."

Theme: Do Good Work

    Not long ago, a friend confided in me about how she hired a company to clean her house. To keep them honest and to double-check their work, she would intentionally place a "dust bunny" on the bedroom floor in the corner of the room. If the cleaning company found the dust bunny and swept it away, then she would hire it; if not, then she wouldn't hire it and tried another company. I used to think this dust bunny technique used as a litmus test to rate a cleaning company's efficiency was crazy. That is, until I started recalling the instances where someone had tried to pass off shoddy work—or no work at all—as a legitimate effort.
    Years ago, I went to breakfast at a well-known national franchise restaurant. I ordered two eggs, harsh browns, and whole wheat toast. At the time, it was late morning, and the restaurant wasn't busy, yet when the waitress served my breakfast it was cold. I complained to the waitress that my breakfast was cold and that I wanted a new one, whereupon she took my plate back to the kitchen. The kitchen had metal swinging doors separating it from the dining room, and when the waitress swung herself through the metal double doors, I saw her place my plate with the cold breakfast on a metal counter to the left inside the door. I watched my cold breakfast plate set on the metal counter for five minutes, then I saw the waitress pick up the cold plate again with my cold breakfast and place the same plate in front of me, as if I had just received a new hot breakfast. I shook my head at her and then asked for the manager. I told the manager what had just happened, and then told him that I'd never set foot in his restaurant or any other restaurant in the franchise again. And, I haven't, although it has been over forty years.
    On another occasion, I bought a new exercise bike at a well-known national appliance store. Unfortunately, when I got the bike home, I discovered that the store had assembled it

incorrectly. For some reason, the lever to activate the various inclines was stuck in the first gear and easiest position. I took the exercise bike back to the Customer Service Counter next to the Service Department, where a very nice assistant manager apologized and promised to fix the bike himself within the hour.

He wheeled the exercise bike away through some double-swinging doors and into the Service Department where I watched it remain untouched for an hour, whereupon the Assistant Manager wheeled it back out to me as if it were as good as new. I told him that I had been sitting for an hour outside the swinging doors leading to the Service Department and that no one had touched the exercise bike. I demanded my money back and he did not dispute my claim. I haven't been back to that appliance store in 50 years, and recently I read in the newspaper that the franchise was on the verge of filing for bankruptcy.

On still another occasion, I bought a newer—yet used—SUV. For years, I have never purchased a new car in order to let someone else take the depreciation hit. I once read a magazine article about buying a new car. It stated that when you buy a new car that it is still a new car until you drive it off the car lot. Once the new car leaves the dealership's lot onto a public street, then it comes a used car, and the car's value immediately plummets $5,000.

On this occasion, I had just bought a two-year-old used SUV, and the salesman told me that all the usual maintenance had been performed on the vehicle, so it was ready for me to drive it home. I lived about four miles from the car dealership, and when I pulled the SUV into my driveway, the "Change Oil" light flashed red on the dashboard. I checked the oil on the engine's dip stick, and the oil was black; it hadn't been changed for a very long time. I took the SUV back to the dealership and spoke to the manager, who apologized and told me that the used SUV had just arrived at the dealership the day before and that there had been a "misunderstanding" about whether the routine maintenance had been completed. The problem with the manager's explanation for the mix-up was that I had seen the same vehicle setting for sale on his car lot for two weeks. In short, his dealership was trying to sell the vehicle without performing any maintenance, although the sticker on the driver's side window indicated that the maintenance had been performed with all the itemized boxes neatly checked, including the oil change box.

These are just a few of the slip-shod work experiences that I have encountered in my lifetime. It seems that not doing your job correctly—or not at all—is okay, if you can get away with it. However, Jesus does not agree. He says that no matter the work that you do in life, do it to the best of your ability and to the "Glory of God." In other words, you're not working for yourself or a company, you're working for God, who demands the very best of your efforts, no matter what work you perform. After all, God gave you the job in the first place, and by doing sub-standard work, you are, in turn, dishonoring Him. He wants you to fulfill your potential, and by doing work that's motivated by laziness and disrespect, you are not doing your part to become a better person nor contributing to making the world a better place. Everything is under God's authority, and that includes the caliber of work you perform. If you do a half-hearted effort you can expect the same from others as well. As they say, "What goes around comes around," and simply doing a job with minimal effort won't move the needle forward towards pleasing God.

Questions
1. Name some instances where you have received sub-standard work?
2. If you didn't complain, why not?
3. If you did complain, was the problem fixed?
4. What caused the sub-standard work in the first place?

17th Century British Literature

Psalms 91:11 "For he shall give his angels charge over thee, to keep thee in all thy ways."

Theme: An Angel Visits

    Years ago, I was required to teach a 17th British Literature course at a small college. I am not a literary scholar, but on occasion I was required to teach a literature course along with my regularly scheduled writing classes. As an English and history major in college, I have always been curious about how people lived and what they thought, so I enjoyed teaching this class because the 17th Century brought about huge changes in people's lives.

    The 17th Century was a huge head-on collision between scientific discovery and religious belief. For example, religion in the 17th Century believed that the earth hung from heaven by a huge Golden Chain, and on that Golden Chain was a Golden Stairway on which angels traveled back-and-forth from heaven. Then Galileo invented the telescope, and people looked through the telescope and didn't see the Golden Chain or the Golden Stairway, so a long-held religious belief was disproved by a scientific invention, which left people questioning their worldview and whether the telescope was an invention of the devil.

    Likewise, in the 21st Century we, too, live in a changing world of scientific disruption. For example, we live in a scientifically defined world comprised of a space/time continuum that states everything has three dimensions: height, width, and depth. Everything that we see and touch in our world has these three basic elements as it occupies space. Therefore, we can see these objects in their space and know their size and shape. In addition, our 3-Dimensional world also has a time element that moves from seconds, to minutes, to hours. Therefore, we can see that the objects exist by their shape and size because they take up space, and we can also know their age by the passing of time.

    However, a 4th dimension also exists, and it is comprised of a spiritual world where the elements are different. For instance, our soul might be temporally housed as seen in our physical 3-D body, but according to some scientists/philosophers our soul resides in an unseen 4th dimension. The 4th dimension doesn't have any measurable 3-D properties like in the world of height, width, or depth; nor does anything in the 4th dimension occupy space. In addition, the 4th dimension also doesn't have the concept of time. Therefore, a soul existing in the 4th dimension can't be seen, measured, or described because it is not physical but spiritual energy that can move limitlessly without the restrictions of time. Some scientists theorize that this is how Jesus could enter a locked room and appear miraculously to His disciples. In short, He simply walked from His spiritually unseen and unrestricted 4th Dimension into our seen and time restricted 3rd Dimension.

In both previous examples, science was used to explain how God's supernatural power works. A simpler explanation—and a Christian one—would be that God can do anything He wants and in any way He wants to do it without explaining Himself to us. It doesn't really matter how God makes supernatural events occur; it is more important that they do occur. People are visited every day by angels; some are seen and appear as people, while others are seen and appear as unworldly dazzling light. All of them are messengers sent to us by God, whether they arrive through a porthole from the 4th dimension or are simply placed on earth by Him, although the invisibility of a 4th dimensional Golden Stairway would certainly explain why Galileo's 3-dimensional telescope couldn't see it.

In the movies and sometimes in life, people readily accept the presence of evil on earth. Most people don't have a problem with envisioning Satan in the world, whether in the form of the devil or demonic possession. The world is a frightening place, perhaps that's why people can so easily accept evil's presence. But the moment that you talk about angels coming to earth to do good, non-believers will call you crazy. Angels don't exist; they don't come to earth and communicate with mortal people. But if we can see Satan's demonic possession at work in the world, then we should also be able to see God's angelic work in the world as well.

Case in point: One Saturday morning just before dawn in

July 1995, I was awakened from a sound sleep by the feeling that there was a presence in my bedroom. I remember sitting up in bed and leaning on my right elbow for support. A figure consisting of millions of tiny stars of dazzling light was standing at the foot of my bed. I remember thinking that I must be asleep and dreaming, so I sat up in bed even further to test this theory. To my surprise, I was totally awake, and a supernatural sparkling figure of light dressed in a robe and hood was standing in my bedroom. I watched the sparkling figure for about 20 seconds and waited to see what it would do. Then the image slowly turned its head towards me and nodded once very slowly. I stared at it for another 10 seconds; then, it gathered itself up into one small glint of light and in a flash disappeared through the glass of my bedroom window. The last time I saw it, it was a v-shaped glint of light disappearing outside in the pre-dawn darkness. Like I said: You tell a story about a supernatural visit from an angel and no one believes you.

Questions
1. Have you ever been visited by a supernatural visitor?
2. Why does man's logic fail to explain God?
3. What was the message that the angel delivered to me?
4. Why are people reluctant to talk about supernatural encounters?

A Miracle

James 5:15-16 "And the prayer of faith shall save the sick.... The effectual fervent prayer of a righteous man availeth much."

Theme: The Power of Prayer

Not long ago, my wife received a telephone call that an 8-year-old boy was in critical condition in the Intensive Care Unit at University of Iowa Hospitals. He had a virus and his brain was swelling to a point where he had gone into a coma. The doctors had done all that they could; many doctors from many different departments had been called in to lend an opinion, but none had the solution. In short, the doctors were out of answers and standing around wringing their hands. They had pooled their collective knowledge and had done all for the boy that they could; subsequently, they prepared the family members for the worst. His death was imminent, and there was no more that the doctors could do. An eyewitness told me his mother was a "basket case" and his father—also a doctor—was no better.

When my wife told me about the condition of the 8-year-old boy, we immediately decided to call the pastor at our church, who immediately contacted the prayer team, who immediately contacted all the church members to pray to the Lord Jesus to heal the boy. Within minutes of my request to our pastor, hundreds of people were praying for the boy's recovery, and the next morning—without warning—the boy sat up in bed and began talking. The swelling on his brain had disappeared and suddenly the boy was his old self again. Furthermore, there weren't any side effects from his brain swelling. No long-term therapy was necessary, and no medication was dispensed. In short, his dire, life-threatening condition had suddenly and without warning disappeared. The doctors could not explain it. And, of course, the parents and family members were elated at the turn of events. The parents had gone from the thoughts of making funeral arrangements for their son to seeing him sitting up in bed and talking, as if nothing had happened to him.

When I called our pastor the next morning to let him know about the sudden reversal of the boy's condition, he related that he and the congregation had been praying fervently for the boy's recovery and that their prayers had been answered and that the Lord Jesus had definitely intervened. In short, the boy's recovery to full health was nothing short of a miracle! The pastor then told me to tell the parents someday about who had recovered their son's health and given him back to them. Yet, when I spoke to an immediate friend of the family, she told me that the parents did not attend church and did not have faith.

Yesterday in the mail, my wife and I received a "Thank You" card from the mother of the boy. She had heard about our prayers and those prayers of the members of our church on her son's behalf. Evidently, she respected our prayer efforts for her son's return to health and the intervention of Jesus to return her son to her. There could be no other explanation: The Lord Jesus had intervened and answered our prayers for her son. It was, indeed, a pure and true miracle!

Questions
1. Do you know of similar miracles? If so, explain them.
2. Does Jesus perform miracles every day that aren't so dramatic. Explain some.
3. Do some people miss Jesus working in their lives? If so, why?
4. Do you think that Jesus saved the boy's life for a reason? What are some of the possible reasons?

The Wedding Date

2 Peter 21 "For it had been better for them not to have known the way of righteousness than, after they have known it, to turn from the holy commandment delivered unto them."

Theme: Abuse of Power

Years ago, when I was teaching at a university, an older student asked me for a one week's absence so that he could get married. I congratulated him on the occasion and then he filled me in on the wedding details. His bride-to-be was from Denmark and spoke only broken English, and his house was now filled with 25 relatives from Denmark who didn't speak any English. Fortunately, the wedding was on Saturday, a few days away, and then they would spend a week in Punta Cana on their honeymoon. One week later, he returned to my college classroom, but he was not elated like I expected him to be. A man, I presumed, just returning from his honeymoon should certainly have a smile on his tanned face, but nothing was further from the truth.

"What's the matter?" I asked. "Didn't the wedding go well?"

"Yes, the wedding went fine," he replied. "The trouble began when we returned from our honeymoon."

When the young bride and groom returned home from their honeymoon in Punta Cana, a letter from the Wisconsin State Treasures Office awaited them. In the official envelop from the State of Wisconsin was their marriage license. It was voided because it had been signed in blue ink instead of black ink. A very obedient Wisconsin State civil servant had taken it upon himself to nullify their marriage because of the color of the ink used to sign the license. Technically, all legal documents in Wisconsin must be signed in black ink for them to be valid.

"So," I said to the young man. "Are you married or not?"

"Yes," he replied." We went down to the Justice of the Peace at the County Court House this morning and got married again."

"When is your wedding anniversary date? Is it on the date when you had the big wedding ceremony? Or, is it today when you said your wedding vows again before the Justice of the

Peace?"

"Oh, we're still going to honor the date of the big wedding ceremony. But what kind of a person would void a marriage license and ruin a marriage ceremony date based on the color of a pen's ink?"

It's true that the bureaucrat had the legal right to rescind the wedding license because of the color of the ink. But isn't it also true that he had the moral obligation not to? How many thousands of legal documents were already signed, on file, and enforced in blue ink at the Wisconsin State Capitol? Blue ink reads just as clearly as black ink and a marriage license is a once-in-a-lifetime document. When voiding the marriage license, the bureaucrat could have probably listed any number of reasons for his decision. "He was just doing his job; he didn't make the law, and he was just following the rules." However, isn't there a higher moral authority that over-rides the power of secular law?

Power corrupts, and few people can handle it with dignity. Even those people who have exercised power for a long time in the end often fail to use it properly, and their improper actions often take hold of an otherwise decent person. Perhaps power corrupts because it is difficult to handle a sacred trust given to them by God. In Exodus 19, God trusted Moses and called him up to Mount Sinai. "…and the Lord called Moses up to the top of Mount; and Moses went up" (Exodus 19:20). In other words, God called Moses up to Mount Sinai to speak to him about relaying His message to the people of Israel on how to behave in a manner pleasing to Him. God trusted Moses with the power to communicate His will to the people. It was a sacred trust between God and Moses, one which God depended on Moses to deliver accurately. Thus, God gave Moses power over the people because he alone would deliver to us The Ten Commandments.

The list of people throughout history who have betrayed their sacred trust with God is too long to mention. In fact, it probably includes most people, although trust is an essential element of power and to human progress and dignity. There's nothing worse than being lied to by someone you trust. And, for sure, we all fall short of the glory of God, but Christians should especially exercise power wisely because they know it is given to them by God. In fact, there is nothing more pathetic than a religious leader who deceives his congregation. If Moses had done this, we would have never received The Ten Commandments. What if Moses had simply discarded The Ten Commandments written on stone tablets because they were too heavy to carry down Mount Sinai? What if Moses at the bottom of the mountain had told the people that he alone now was their new god? Moses could have abused his power given to him by God, but he didn't because he knew that his power stemmed from God and that it was a sacred trust.

Today, the responsibility of power given to someone by God is no less sacred. A civil servant who is also a Christian and who lives in the spirit would not have rejected my student's marriage license because the signatures were written in blue ink instead of black ink. A Christian living in the spirit has a higher moral authority—God—than the laws of a secular world. On the day that the bureaucrat rejected my student's marriage license, there were thousands of other documents signed in blue ink on that day being enforced by the laws of the State of Wisconsin. In the case of the debunked marriage license, only God can undo a sacred ceremony conducted in His sight and in His church. The bureaucrat, in my opinion, will someday have to answer for his legalistic actions that defied God and disavowed His trust in a sacred ceremony.

Questions
1. Name some secular laws that are morally wrong?
2. Relate your own stories done to you by a legalistic bureaucrat.
3. Whose law does a Christian living in the spirit follow?
4. If the marriage license had been received by another bureaucrat, would it have been rejected?

American Literature with Walt Whitman

Romans 13:11 "…now it is high time to awake out of sleep: for now is our salvation nearer than when we believed."

Theme: Salvation's Small Steps

    The adage that there is no substitute for experience in life has often applied to me. I have often learned how to do things by watching them being done. However, these tasks usually took place as a physical process like how to change the oil in my car. However, there is a knowledge that I have attained without understanding how it occurred. One instance would be the intellectual ability of how to critically analyze something. It takes place almost like osmosis; it's a creeping process that slowly enters your consciousness because it must be internalized to be understood. Learning to think critically takes place very subtly over a long period of time. In fact, it takes place so slowly that you're learning how to do it by such small steps that you don't even realize that you're learning it. Then a circumstance presents itself to use it, and you suddenly discover that you have a new ability.

    When I was an undergraduate student, I had to take an American Literature course. The course was taught by a professor who everyone characterized as an old scold. I knew of his reputation for being tough before going into the class, but I needed a course at that time and day of the week because it complemented my other scheduled classes. However, it didn't take me long to figure out that this literature class wasn't for me. The first author that we studied was Walt Whitman and his poem "Leaves of Grass." At the time, I thought that I could read and analyze anything. Then Walt Whitman showed up and proved differently. I dropped the class during the first week and took a night class to supplement the other classes on my schedule. Eventually, I went on to graduate with my undergraduate degree without Walt Whitman.

    Then I spent two years in the US Army, and after being discharged from the army I found myself in graduate school needing the same American Literature Walt Whitman class. I registered for the class, and to my surprise the class was being taught by the same scold of a professor and in the very same classroom. On the first day of class, I sat down at the same desk that I had occupied two years prior, and when the professor entered the classroom, he had the same stone-faced look, and I thought "Here we go again."

Yet, on that first day when the professor started to read verses from Walt Whitman's "Leaves of Grass," a miraculous thing happened to me. I not only clearly understood what Walt Whitman was saying, but his words were also earth-shatteringly beautiful. What had happened to me in the past two years that I now could understand and appreciate Walt Whitman's poetry? The only event coming between Whitman, this class, and me during the past two years was the US Army. During that time, the army had somehow changed me and had given me insight about life that enabled me to now understand Walt Whitman's work.

Similarly, I believe that Jesus's gift of salvation also works slowly and invisibly as well. Through the small and sometimes ordinary events of our life, the Lord Jesus works in our hearts to help us to piece together our salvation. Many people longing for salvation often wait for The Big Moment when it arrives. However, I suspect that the arrival of salvation through the Lord Jesus Christ is more subtle and heartfelt. Life-changing events usually take place in intricate and unrecognizable pieces over time, and sometimes even the moment of our salvation gets clouded in the clamor of life. Yet, Jesus is at work in your life and in your heart to bring you to Him.

However, one thing is for sure: Nothing leading to your salvation happens by chance; the Lord Jesus purposely places the events leading to your salvation in your life's path. Many salvation scenarios might go something like this: At first, you might feel an emptiness and longing for something better in your life. Then, someone might give you a Bible. Or, perhaps you find one left on a park bench by someone directed by Jesus to leave it there for you. But a Christian knows that nothing in this world connected to salvation occurs by accident. Then one Sunday Jesus directs you into a church not far from your house. Your neighbors have invited you there many times, but you were always too busy to attend. Then Jesus tugs at your heart and places you at the church's front door.

To non-believers, all these small and ordinary occurrences in life happen randomly. But to a Christian, when Jesus Christ is working on your heart no occurrence is small or inconsequential when it comes to your salvation; it might seem so, but it isn't. To a Christian, all actions—even the smallest—are directed by God to have meaning and are interconnected by Jesus to combine with other actions to create a salvation chain of events. I don't know all the events in my life that eventually brought me to Jesus and to my salvation. Only Jesus knows all of them because He has known me since the foundation (creation) of the world. And because He knows his own, He will eventually bring His own to Him.

Questions
1. As best as you can, explain the events in your own life that led you to your own salvation.
2. Recall one seemingly random occurrence that you now understand as significant.
3. Explain how one person in your life has made a huge difference in accepting Jesus as your Lord and Savior.
4. Describe the emptiness in your heart before your salvation.
5. How has your life changed because of your salvation?

The Church at Easter

Ecclesiastes 3:1 "To every thing there is a season, and a time to every purpose under the heaven:"

Theme: Spiritual Messaging

Recently, while on vacation I attended church on Easter Sunday. The church was unknown to me, and there wasn't a lot of time to research the churches to attend. I was on vacation with my family, and we had just flown into town the night before. In fact, it was my son-in-law who after some cursory internet investigation found our family a church close by our rental house to attend.

We arrived at our unknown church to discover that the church was new and by our standards large. It had over 2,000 members—mostly 30ish couples with young children. We arrived a few minutes late, and we were escorted by an usher to our seats in the third row. It was dark inside the church, especially after arriving on a bright, sunny day and with the inside of the church being dimly lighted. In short, we were in the dark about our environment. Then suddenly, a thunderous drum roll sounded, strobe lights of many colors started flashing, and to my surprise eight young men—dressed in black pants and black shirts—started doing back-flips across the stage. Then some white spotlights highlighted the stage and swirled in circles around the worship team musicians in an expectant manner. Two drummers, two organists, a saxophone player, a bass guitarist, a lead guitarist and four singers, including the pastor who sang lead vocal, broke into a frenzy of thunderous and deafening music as all instruments and vocalists collided in an amplified sound supplied by eight twenty-foot high speakers. When the people doing back-flips across the stage started, my 30-year-old daughter turned to me amid the noise as if to say, "What in the world is this?" Then, she covered the ears of her 15-month old baby with the palms of her hands and handed her to my wife who took her to the lobby. The pastor -- grey-haired, beer-bellied, and dressed in a flowered Hawaiian shirt -- should have left the singing to the other singers on the worship team. He sang flat and out of key but was the center of attention. When the huge video screens on the walls finished individually highlighting the band members during their performance, a 10-minute video followed showing the pastor screaming while riding in the backseat of an open cock pit of a dare devil airplane doing barrel rolls. No connection was made—or could be made—between the barrel-rolling airplane, the pastor's screaming, and the content of the sermon.

The sermon focused lightly upon the Easter message of Jesus' resurrection, and the pastor did not instruct anyone to open their Bible to scripture or instructed anyone to find a Bible in the back of the seat in front of them. In fact, as I looked around no one was carrying a Bible. Evidently, a Bible wasn't necessary because the pastor kept them entertained on stage. During his sermon, he punched holes into a Styrofoam cup with a pin to demonstrate how nothing but Jesus can fill up your life. He smashed a full-length mirror with a hammer to shatter our earthly possessions written on the mirror, and he told joke after joke during his sermon much like a stand-up comic. To me, it seemed like the pastor was the focus of the Easter message instead of Jesus. I admit that it's better that people attended any kind of Easter Service rather than not attend one at all, although the antics and theatrics seemed to me to dilute the resurrection message instead of amplifying it.

Overall, the Easter service consisted of 5 percent message and 95 percent entertainment. Granted, God loves someone with a sense of humor; otherwise, why would He have given us one. Yet, there is a time and a place for serious contemplation, and to confuse the seriousness of the Easter's message with cheap theatrical stunts was misguided. God didn't have comedy in mind when he rose His only Son Jesus from the tomb and resurrected Him from death into life so that we, too, could experience that same spiritual resurrection upon our own physical death. To me, the transformation upon my death from living in a physical body to living in a spiritual body with Jesus in Heaven is no laughing matter.

Questions
 1. Have you ever attended a church service much

different from your own church? Explain.
2. Does how a church explain the gospel matter? Why?
3. Why do some churches use theatrics?
4. What kind of theatrics subtract rather than add to the spiritual message?

Ancestral Heritage

Micah 2:2 "...so they oppress a man and his house, even a man and his heritage."

Theme: On Recreating History

At daybreak on July 7, 1863, the Union Army attacked a Confederate camp at Gladeville, Virginia. Most of the Confederate soldiers were captured while still asleep in tents and others barricaded themselves in the Gladeville Courthouse and eventually surrendered. Some Confederate officers were rounded up in the village while sleeping overnight in residential homes after attending a dance the previous evening. The result was that 123 Confederate soldiers were captured, put into horse-drawn wagons, and transported to a Camp Chase, which was a Union POW camp near Columbus, Ohio. One first-person eyewitness newspaper account stated, "After the skirmish was over, we got our prisoners together. We found that we had 123, and of the number about 20 were commissioned officers." ("The Raid On Gladeville, July 7, 1863" by P.M. Redding, McLaughlin Squadron of Ohio, Vagabond Gazette, July 1930.)

I mention this Civil War skirmish because one of those 123 captured Confederate prisoners was my great-grandfather, Pvt. William Riley Shepherd. My great-grandfather would spend the next two and one-half years in the POW camp, and he would leave the POW camp with severe liver and kidney problems because of poor food and lack of sanitary conditions. I know this because after The Civil War federal documents state that he received a US Government pension for his injuries, yet despite his war injuries, my great-grandfather lived to be 95 years old.

My great-grandfather Shepherd's ancestry, and now mine, dates back to 1640 when William Shepherd and Mary Shepherd, his wife, came by sea from England to Maryland as indentured servants, who would work for a Mr. Teague for five years in exchange for land in America. My Shepherd descendants and their heritage is registered in Maryland and Virginia as one of America's oldest families. I am an 11th generation Shepherd, and along the way in my family history there have been scoundrels and heroes. But my point is that it is my heritage and it should not be rewritten; it should be truthfully preserved for the next generation because it is their heritage, too. We cannot and should not take responsibility for our ancestors' actions; they were them, and we are us. And we should not rewrite history and our ancestors' role in it to conveniently and politely revise its meaning; instead, we should protect our heritage by defending our descendants' right to live their life as they saw it in their historical time.

Micah 2:2 addresses the wicked deeds of the rich in relationship to heritage. Like in most periods of history, the rich exploited the poor by taking their crops, land, and houses by violent means. In Micah 2:2, however, Micah states that the rich took "…even a man and his heritage." So, it wasn't enough for the rich to take the tangible goods of hard work like crops and houses; the rich were also intent on taking a man's right to anything by birth inherited by legal succession. In short, the rich wanted to eradicate any descendants and heirs to make their deeds to the spoils indisputable.

If a person doesn't know his heritage, then he doesn't have any expectation regarding the passing on of property. It is the end of the line for both ancestry and inheritance. To sever someone's legal right to property is cruel, but to sever someone's right to their own bloodline seems unfathomable. Every person who exists today needs to acknowledge their long line of ancestral progression that preceded their birth. Simply put, without those ancestors, you would not exist! The Father of all of us, of course, is God in heaven, and he has always known that your life would exist and when. And He also knew the progression of ancestral events that would lead to your birth. So, by wiping the ancestral slate clean in Micah 2:2, the rich have ceased to allow someone to know how God planned a person to get here. It is this opposition against God's ancestral intent that is the grave sin. To oppose God for your own greed is never a good move, especially when His most precious possession on earth are those sheep that know His voice.

After the Civil War ended, my great-grandfather was released from the POW camp and returned home. Yet, he often talked about the rich and fertile Ohio farmland that he had seen. The Ohio farmland was certainly better than the hard scrabble soil in the hill country on the border between Kentucky and Virginia. Eventually, some Shepherd family members became curious about the fertile Ohio farmland and migrated to Ohio to get a look for themselves. One of those curious Shepherds was my grandfather, who became a sharecropper there, and bore a son—my father in Montgomery, Ohio. Later, my father would move to southern Michigan to find work and meet my mother, and that's where I was born.

Therefore, understanding your family's heritage is essential to understanding who you are and where you came from because your heritage and its progression is God's hand at work. God has made your ancestry gene pool for a reason, and the gene pool is very deep. In my case, He has placed all eleven generations of my Shepherd family members exactly where He wanted them to be and when. Right now, I'm sitting at my kitchen table in my house in Cedar Rapids, Iowa—exactly where I am supposed to be—and writing about the importance of heritage, as related in Micah 2:2, so that God can convey that important message to you.

Questions
1. How many generations back can you name your ancestors?
2. What personality traits do you have that mirror your parents?
3. God controls everything; therefore, why is it important to know your heritage?
4. What personality and physical traits has God passed on to your children through you?

God: The Power Source of Everything

Matthew 28:18 "All power is given unto me in heaven and in earth."

Theme: Soul Authority

    In just my lifetime, society has drastically changed. I grew up in the 1950's and 1960's. When I tell my college students that my house was the first one in my neighborhood to have a television, they don't believe me. They especially don't believe me when I tell them that the television programing was only on for three hours per day—one hour in the morning and two hours in the evening. In fact, I remember watching the Test Pattern on the television and waiting for the programming to start. The Test Pattern was a circular line drawing of the profile of an Indian chief, complete with headdress. In addition, my household also had one of the first telephones in the neighborhood. It was one of those Elliot Ness 1930's models with two parts where you had to place the earpiece to your ear to hear. In our house, it set on a Duncan Phyfe mahogany table in the living room. I was three years old when I saw my mother answer it one morning and start to cry. My grandfather had died suddenly from a heart attack. Our telephone had a party line, which meant that three or four other families shared the same telephone number. So, you could pick up the telephone to make a call and someone else would be talking on it. You could announce that your call was an emergency, and they might hang up so you could use it. Or, someone might just listen in to your conversation just because he or she had nothing else to do. A long-distance call cost so much that it was an earthquake of an occasion. No matter what you were doing, you dropped it to run to the telephone to take the call. A telephone never travelled with you; it was secured to a wall in your house.
    If you wanted to take a photograph, it was usually for a special occasion because a photograph took a long time. First, you had to buy a camera. It was usually a Kodak Brownie camera. You could buy it at the local drug store. While you were at the drug store, you might as well pick up a couple of

rolls of film to load into your camera. A roll of film would take 12 photographs. Then, after you've taken your pictures and used the roll sparingly for several different occasions—some so far apart that you couldn't remember the occasion—then you needed to make another trip to the drug store so that the drug store clerk could send out your rolls of film in the mail to a laboratory to be developed, which usually took about two weeks.

When the photographs returned from the laboratory after they were developed, you had to return to the drug store to pick them up. The black-and-white photographs were usually housed in a little yellow jacket that held them together like a small booklet. The size of the photographs was all the same 3 ½ inches by 3 ½ inches. Any time photographs were enlarged required repeating the process, although few people bothered because enlargements were so expensive and nothing in life was usually that important. Sometimes you'd get the photographs from the laboratory, and the photograph didn't offer any clues as to why you took it. The Kodak Brownie didn't have a zoom lens. So, the photograph of the squirrel sitting on the fence post could just as easily have been a photograph of the house in the background.

Back then, almost everyone smoked cigarettes. They were 25 cents a pack and doctors said that smoking was good for you. Actors in the movies smoked. Even James Bond smoked cigarettes, and who was cooler than him. Cigarette advertisements were everywhere. If the Marlboro man wasn't puffing on a hoofer while riding on his horse into the sunset, then it was the Virginia Slims woman lighting up while sunbathing next to the swimming pool. Smoking cigarettes was a national past time. Car ash trays were full of unfiltered cigarette butts, as well as numerous ash trays throughout the house. People smoked just about anywhere where oxygen could sustain the striking of a match. Later, of course, all that nicotine sophistication would give way to emphysema, COPD, oxygen tanks, and "Why didn't somebody tell me?"

Nobody exercised back then. If someone in my neighborhood was running on the street, he was fleeing the police after just robbing the corner liquor store. High cholesterol didn't even register in America's bloodstream yet, and a beer belly was mistaken for a healthy sign of a good lifestyle. The point is this: things do change around us, but the human condition does not. Today, you don't have to run to your house to answer the telephone; it just calls you from your own pocket, and people often take instant selfie photographs, as if they had forgotten what they looked like. Yet, the chaos of an ever-changing technological society ultimately doesn't change the human condition at all. The basic human questions about life and death are much more complicated than the latest digital device. These complicated questions relate to the state of the human soul and how it translates into our relationship with God. Regardless of the century, people have always been fragile and insecure because they are just deteriorating flesh headed towards a known commitment with death, which can either be a welcoming reunion with God or an eternity with those other souls who gnash their teeth in hell. Either way, our death won't be changed by what type of telephone we use or by the process of developing a photograph. It will, however, be changed by our relationship with Jesus Christ, our Lord and Savior; by confessing our sins and our need for a Savior, by reading God's Word in the Bible, and by listening to the Holy Spirit within us. God is not just a global network; He is the universe's network and the ultimate airwave, satellite, GPS, and power source of everything. Not connecting with God, who is the ultimate source of power, will prevent people from tuning into their own individual human power, which is God's plan for them on earth. Without connecting with God, who is the power source of everything, you will know little about the truth of your own existence.

Discussion Questions
1. Name some technological changes that have taken place during your lifetime.
2. Have any of these changes influenced how God conducts salvation?
3. Do you think that access to a computer has helped or hurt Christianity?
4. Do you read the Bible on-line? Or, do you still carry a hard copy of the Bible? Is God's word the same in both?

Other titles from Higher Ground Books & Media:

Wise Up to Rise Up by Rebecca Benston

A Path to Shalom by Steen Burke

Overcomer by Forrest Henslee

Miracles: I Love Them by Forest Godin

32 Days with Christ's Passion by Mark Etter

Knowing Affliction and Doing Recovery by John Baldasare

Out of Darkness by Stephen Bowman

The Magic Egg by Linda Phillipson

The Tin Can Gang by Chuck David

Whobert the Owl by Mya C. Benston

Add these titles to your collection today!

http://highergroundbooksandmedia.com

Do you have a story to tell?

Higher Ground Books & Media is an independent Christian-based publisher specializing in stories of triumph! Our purpose is to empower, inspire, and educate through the sharing of personal experiences.

Please visit our website for our submission guidelines.

http://www.highergroundbooksandmedia.com

www.ingramcontent.com/pod-product-compliance
Lightning Source LLC
Chambersburg PA
CBHW020007050426
42450CB00005B/347